TRACE YOUR
GERMAN
ROOTS ONLINE

KELBV...

Rostock · Molchin · Anclam · Treptow
Neustat · Trauemund · Wismar · Demin · Newbrä: de: borg · Pase: walck
Itzeho · Neumüster · Lubec · MECA · Waren
Ritzbuttel · Fengenb: · Hamborg · Gustrow · Plauen · Wesen: berg
Ritzen: · Otered · Oldesfloe · Sweri · Parch: im · Newstadt · Zedeniz
Berg: kesa · Staden · Lawen: borg · Wöln · Witteborg · Lubicz · Furſteberg
Stotel · Vorden · Bewezenborg · Domicz · Parleberg · Witstock · Angermund
Ezes · Jeuer · Mol · Lunenborg · Albs fl · Dannen: berg · Wiſſenack · MARCA · Graſſoe · Neſtat
Norden · Fredebo · Bremen · Vlczen · Oſterborg · Schuſen · Nawen: berg Bocſow · Pernow · Frien wold
Emden · Haſelingen · Verden · Alden · Zeel · Soltwedel · Warpen · Hau: elberg · Ratenaw · Berlin · Mönchel berg
SIA · Oldenborch · Delm: horſt · Aller A · Burgdorf · Garleben · Tangermund · Spädau · Kope: nick · Furſten walt
FRI · Groningen · Niebus · Cloppen: borch · Wil huſe · Hove · Brau: nſwig · Stendel · NO · dichorg · Brau: · Beliz · Beſke
Groningen · Lin: gen · Quak: enbrugge · Witlag · Nienborg · Leim A · Hanofer · Helmſtat · Mag: de borg · Zerbſt VA · Luben · Luca · Corbus
Campen · Herden: berg · Northorn · Osſen: brug · Minden · Hern: ont · Hildesheim · Halberſtat · Wittenberg · LYZATIA · Schlieben · Hertzberg
Vollen houe · Deuenter · Almelo · Rene · Lengow · Hame: len · Goslar · SAXO · Hall · NI · Dibe · Finſterwald
WESTFALIA · Engern · Boden werd · Gandersham · Stalberg · Eisleben · Torga · Strelin · Camicz
Emerich · Munſter · Bilfeld · Ravensburg · Brakel · Nort: huſen · Hanſuelt · Leypzig · els · Grun · Balzen
CLI · Weſel · Coſſelt · Tecklen: borg · Huren · Northeim · Sunderhuſen · TVRING · Weil · Naw: burg · MISNIA · Meiſſen
Cleue · Dorsten · Ham · Lippe · Palborn · Boden werd · Gottingen · IA · Iena · Alden: burg · Cnem: itz · Dresden · Pirn
VIA · Eſſen · Suſt · Werla Geisko · Warborg · Hunden · Erffurt · Gotha · Weida · Salfeld · Zuickaw · Shneberg · Auſſic
GEL · Gelder · Vnna · Dortmund · HAS · Ferſler · Caſſel · Capel · Crutzberg · Isnach · Ilmenaw · Solburk · Hock · Obnicz · Anneberg · Leutin
DRIA · Roer: mont Nus · Leney · Aittendorn · Waldeck · Dreis · Homburg · Spangeberg · Vach · Aurſperch · Eiſffelt · Plauen · Shiveberg
Gulick · Coelen · Sigen · Marpurg · Cronberg Hirſfeldt · SIA · Fuld · Neuſtat · Coburg · Schweinfurt · Haſfurt · Staffelſtein · Iochins: tal · Laun · Veron
Duren · kerpen · Bon · Lintz · Dillemberg · Gieſſen · Buzbach · Gelnhauſen · Hamelnpurg · Hasfurt · Culmbach · Eger Elzpogen · Sacz · Piſſen
Reimbach · Andernach · Wielmuſt · Weilburg · Frideberg · Gemund · Neuſt: at · Haſlach · Bamberg · Potenſtain · Deutſchen Reid · Dachaun · BOHE
Drim: born · Cobelents · Boppart · Gwer · Wefel · Ments · Wert: heim · Wirtzburg · Kitzing · CO · Forchaim · Benaw · Neumarck
Alten Arburg Aar · Sümeren · Francfort · Geraw · Darstat · Miltenburg · Rotingen · AN · Onsbach · Herſpruck · Taindo · Neumarck
XEL · Virnburg · S Gwer · Oppen: um · Creutz: nach · Heidelberg · Wimpfen · FR · Rotenburg · Nurenberg · Weiden · Wald: munch · Glatta · Suſiez
Bitzburg · Bergcaſtel · Binge · Wornbs · Hall · Onsbach · NIA · Am: berg · Chamb · Koczing
Ettel: ruck · Treir · Kirberg · Lutreck · Leiningen · Keiſers: lanterē · Speir · Veccar fl · Canſtat · Dinken: ſpuhel · Guntzen: hauſen · Neuburg · Lengenfelt · Kru
HA · Zarbruck · Freu: denberg · Kuſſtel · Zwei: brucken · Weiſſen: burg · Rhein: zab: ern · Aſcherg · Weiſſen: burg · Neumarck · Kelheim · Straubingē · Teckendo: rf
Valken: brug · Bitſch · Raſtat · Pfortzen · Stukgart Eslingen · Norlin: gen · Aichſtet · Regensburg · Paſſaw
Vinſtingen · Hagenaw · Bade · Wildbat · WIRTEN: Tu: bingen · Geppingen · Ingolſtat · Mieck: mul · Mieuburg · Vilſhouen
Numein · Wich · Zabern · Straſburg · BERG · Blauhuren · Rotenburg · Donaw fl · Neuſtat · Iſere · Eckefeld · Scherding
ALSATIA · Offenburg · Dornheim · SVE · Vlm · Burgaw · Kindfelt · Landſhut · Otingen · Brunau · Ried
Lienſtat · Blancken: burg · Tanbach · Rinow · Babling · V · Zusmar: hauſen Augſpurg · Dach: aun · Arding · Senus fl · Burck hauſen · Feckelb
S.Didbolt · Schleſtat · Retwijl · Riedlin: gē · Biberach · I · Dachaun · Munchen · Waſſer burg · Freiberg · S.W
Rauon · Colmar · Briſach · Greſin: gen · Ochſenhuſen · A · Lands: berg · Carls: berg · Delcz · Salczburg · Ruchel
Bruier · Rufach · Fribur · Vberin: gen · Memingen · Fuſſē · Ail: bling · VA · Roſen: haim · Reichenh al · Werben
Spital · Dan · Badenwiler · Schafhuſen · Yſna Kemptē · Weil: ben · Kopfſtein · Kickz: buhel · Biſchoſs · S.Vit
Blumer · Baſel · Coſtenz · Lindau · Eren: berg · Schwacz · S.Vit
Mönpel: gart · Mulhuſen · Lauffen: berg · Frauwefel · Bregentz · RIA · Brandſtet
Blumberg · HEL · Baden · Zurich · Phludencz · Hall · Gaſtein · Raſtat
Clareual · Witzelspach · A den fu: se · Lichten: ſteg · Sefelt · Inſpruck
Landeri · Zur ſe · Zug · Ri: Feldt: Kloſter: Stams
ſanſon · Arbera · Solothurn · Einſideln · ua · kirch · lin · Katra

TRACE YOUR GERMAN ROOTS ONLINE

A Complete Guide
to German Genealogy Websites

JAMES M. BEIDLER

FAMILY
TREE
BOOKS

Cincinnati, Ohio
shopfamilytree.com

CONTENTS

PART ONE: GERMAN GENEALOGY BASICS

Kick-start your genealogical journey with this chapter's information about the basics of German research and the *Bundesrepublik Deutschland*.

Learn the dos and don'ts of online German genealogy. This chapter will outline key Web resources and help you set realistic expectations for your research.

Decode your ancestors' garbled name and place of origin with these translation tools and keys to understanding botched German spelling and phonetics.

PART TWO: TOP GERMAN GENEALOGY WEBSITES

Explore the Internet's largest free resource for family records. This chapter unpacks the more than 50 million German records housed by FamilySearch.org.

Pinpoint your ancestors' records in the vast collection of databases held by Ancestry.com and its affiliate sites. This chapter unpacks what the world's largest genealogy website can do for you.

Discover what the German (Genealogy.net) and English (GenWiki) versions of this valuable resource can offer you.

Scour MyHeritage's vast collection of family trees for information about your own German ancestors.

Master Archion's invaluable collection of Protestant church records from across modern Germany.

INTRODUCTION

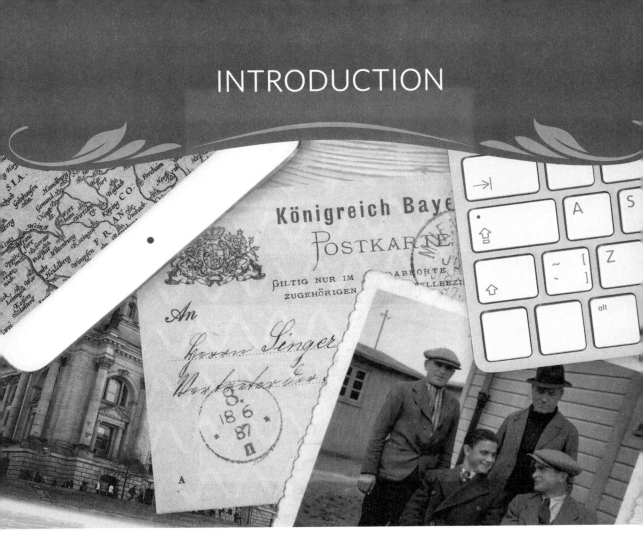

began my genealogical quest in the Gutenberg age: the one in which you methodically produced pedigree and family group charts on paper, waited sometimes months or years for someone to answer a query, and put the greatest stock in the monthly meetings of your local genealogical society.

But my quest continues in the digital age in which family trees can be shared globally, communication can be instant, and many "meetings" are virtual linkups called webinars. While some nostalgia remains for the "good ol' days," that sense is overwhelmed by the enormity of information, often freely available, right on a computer desktop.

This book is a product of the realization that German genealogy has reached a tipping point in the journey from Gutenberg to digital. An irony of this process is that many Gutenberg-age products—books and newspapers—are no less important to the genealogist today than they were back then; it's just that their format and accessibility has changed radically as the information has been made available through scanned digital images (in the case of historical paper documents) and as more resources have been "born digital" in today's electronic environment.

One of my first inklings that such a tipping point was coming happened in 2002 when I was haunting Internet genealogy bulletin boards in an effort to find information on a family named Rauch—more specifically, on Gertraut, a woman who one of my Rauch ancestors married but whose maiden name I couldn't find any evidence for. She was one of several female ancestors for which I had the "tease" of an exact birth date (this one in 1770) but no clue in any later records linking her to her family before her marriage to Jacob Rauch.

Within hours of my inquiry post, a researcher named DelLynn Leavitt from Idaho Falls, Idaho, replied that he knew that she was the daughter of Jacob Sicher. With that, the power of Internet research was proven to me without a doubt as it brought together researchers who were geographically far apart. Correspondence with this researcher, as well as articles he's posted on the Internet, also led to several further generations in my Rauch line itself, including pushing my family tree back to the town of origin in Europe, which is almost always the Holy Grail for genealogical researchers. Of course, I was ecstatic at these finds, but DelLynn kind of shrugged it off: "I do enjoy helping other people out," he said. "And most of my best leads lately have come from individuals who I have helped out at one time or another and are returning the favor."

Now, more than a dozen years later, one of my motivations for writing this book is to return his favor and many others I've received over the years. It is my hope that this book will enable its readers to open virtual doors that reveal further information about their German ancestry and allow them the great satisfaction that comes with a long *Deutsch* pedigree.

James M. Beidler

<www.jamesmbeidler.com>
Leesport, Pennsylvania

PART ONE

GERMAN GENEALOGY BASICS

1

BEGINNING YOUR GERMAN RESEARCH

Just five years ago, devoting an entire book to online sources for genealogists with German-speaking ancestors wouldn't have been a particularly fulfilling exercise. Relatively few genealogical problems could be solved "beginning to end" on either German- or American-based websites.

But oh, what a difference those five years have made. Whether it's the "big kahunas" of the online genealogy world, such as FamilySearch.org <www.familysearch.org> and Ancestry.com <www.ancestry.com>, adding more German content, the digitization of church registers that play such an important role for this ethnic group, or any of the other solutions the Web has provided to the myriad genealogy questions that arise—the availability of Internet sources for German research has come of age.

HOW TO GET THE MOST OUT OF THIS BOOK

You've no doubt already heard that more people in America claim German ancestry than they do any other ethnic heritage. What that means in practical terms is that more digitized records, more databases, and more how-to guides exist for German ancestry than for any other ethnicity. Add that to the fact that Germans have been scrupulously keeping some types of records for centuries, and you have a recipe for success. The Internet is full of resources for those researching German ancestry, and we'll cover many of them in this book.

This Book's Scope

The scope of *Trace Your German Roots Online* includes both American and European websites, and there's a good reason for this: In many—if not most—cases, you haven't been handed an ancestral line all the way back into Europe. Even if you know the name of an immigrant ancestor, you may not know the immigrant's village of origin, which is crucial for further research. And even if you've found a name for the village of origin in an American record, it's likely to have been garbled in some way that makes further research impossible until you've unraveled it. Records generated in America are often the ticket to working through this process.

In addition, this book aims to help family history researchers who are seeking German-speaking ancestors (pre- and post-immigration) through websites with records and information from both sides of the Atlantic. That identifier is a bit too lengthy to keep using throughout, so instead, let's resolve now that phrases such as *German researchers*, *German genealogy*, and *German genealogical sources* apply to this group.

This Book's Format

Whether these most common of queries—such as finding the name of the village of origin, then finding its "real," native name—or one of the many that follow, questions can best be solved by observing how you frame them. And for that reason, this book uses the questions most applicable to German genealogists as jumping-off points for many of its chapters. As you'll see, after you get your feet wet in part 1 with the basics of German genealogy, part 2 lists the top websites that virtually every researcher will need, and these sites will help answer many of those questions. Then part 3 will cover more focused, niche sites to help you answer single, specialized questions.

GETTING BACK TO BASICS

People start doing genealogy in many ways and for many reasons, but successful family historians usually follow the same general practices. While other resources will dive into more detail about these strategies, this section will give you an overview of some general genealogical research strategies that you'll likely find helpful.

◼ Work Backward in Time

Especially when wanting to connect their ancestry with a famous person, many people are tempted to just look for a family pedigree (either in old-fashioned book form or as one of the burgeoning collaborative Internet trees—more on these in chapter 2) to see if they match up with that family. Resist that temptation, because it's usually a waste of time. Better, instead, to work backward in time—from the known to unknown—by starting with whatever documents, photos, and writings you have in your family, then interviewing relatives to find out more as you go back.

◼ Evaluate and Cite Sources

Knowing where your information comes from and how reliable it is forms the bedrock of any good research. Regardless of where you're searching, you'll want to learn to cite sources so others can understand how you arrive at your conclusions about identities, dates, and relationships, if and when you share your findings (and you will understand your own methodology when you later review your earlier work). Part of this attention to sources involves an appreciation for the different tiers of research.

In the past decade, the professional genealogy world, led by the Board for Certification of Genealogists (BCG) **<www.bcgcertification.org>**, has put forth a sophisticated method for evaluating resources. Under these guidelines, sources are either *original* or *derivative*, and the information shown in them is either *primary* or *secondary*. The resulting evidence stemming from that information is then either *direct* or *indirect*. An excellent explanation of these terms appears in the article "Skillbuilding: Guidelines for Evaluating Genealogical Resources" on the BCG website **<www.bcgcertification.org/skillbuilders/skbld085.html>**.

◼ Recognize Time and Place

The time in which your ancestor lived and the place or places where he resided are like a set of crosshairs that help determine what types of records you have the potential to find. Learning the history of your ancestor's residences enables you to avoid pitfalls related to changes in governmental boundaries, which have an impact on where you'll find documents ranging from wills to deeds to tax records. Where your ancestors lived also determines what records were even kept for a particular time period.

▲ Practice "Whole Family Genealogy"

Yes, of course your direct-line ancestors are the most interesting to you. But branching out to research your direct ancestors' siblings will help you learn more about those direct-line ancestors. For instance, your ancestor's death certificate might have only slashes for her mother's name, but the certificates of her siblings may name her.

▣ Stay Organized

Keep track of your genealogy with pedigree charts (showing your direct line back from parents to grandparents to great-grandparents, etc.) and family group sheets (listing a couple and their children). Genealogy software programs automate this process. Another tool for presenting your information—which, again, software will generate—is the German-originated *Ahnentafel* (literally, "ancestor table"), a compact way of showing all your ancestors. In this scheme, you (or whatever person closest in time you're starting with—say, your child) are No. 1, your father is No. 2, and your mother is No. 3. Then each preceding generation follows, with the father's number being double that of the child's and the mother's being "double plus one" of the child's.

GERMANY AT A GLANCE

A common theme of research is that you'll need to learn about the country you're researching in, and that definitely applies here. No study of how to research German genealogy would be complete without a crash course in German history and culture. This section will briefly discuss the historical and political divisions of Germany as well as which religious denominations were prevalent in German culture and how they shaped its history. In addition to providing more insight into your ancestors' lives, this information will help you track down civil and church records in your research.

Historical and Modern Political Divisions of Germany

Today's Federal Republic of Germany (*Bundesrepublik Deutschland*) is a union of sixteen *Länder* (the plural of *Land*, the German equivalent of an American state), a fair number of which have no historical significance since they do not predate World War II. The *Länder* are made up of districts or *Kreise* (singular: *Kreis*), which are more or less the same level of government as American counties. Significant municipal mergers in the 1960s and 1970s in Germany resulted in some newly created village names. For example,

Hachenbach and Niedereisenbach, two historically separate villages on either side of the Glan River, were combined as *Glanbrücken*, a name not previously used.

Loads of mostly tiny German states existed for hundreds of years. Even though the number of these states was drastically reduced in the European reorganization after Napoleon Bonaparte's defeat in 1815, many people today still retain regional affinities. More important, you must think of a village's political allegiance both historically and in modern times to determine where to find all relevant records. For example, the university city of Heidelberg was the off-and-on capital of the Electoral Palatinate for centuries. In the nineteenth century, it became part of Baden, which is now part of the *Land* Baden-Württemberg. You will find records relating to Heidelberg, therefore, at archives in both the Palatinate (now part of the *Land* Rhineland-Palatinate) and Baden.

The upshot of this anything-but-linear division, redivision, and amalgamation of political units is that you need to always challenge your assumptions about where you might find records relating to your ancestor—and as a consequence, which repositories' websites will have the relevant information. For better or worse, we'll give you even more detail how to figure this out in chapter 9.

Religion in Germany

Here's a short comparison: In the United States, we have a whole Baskin-Robbins store of religious flavors, while in Germany, you've pretty much got vanilla and chocolate.

OK, it's not quite that simple—once Germans hit America, they become part of that kaleidoscope of religious freedom that has resulted in a plethora of Christian denominations, but that religious diversity was not always as significant in the old country. Let's start with the simplicity of Germany today and work backward to the complications.

Today in Germany, most of the churches where your ancestors worshipped are either Roman Catholic (*Katholisch*) or Protestant (*Evangelisch* which translates poorly into English as "Evangelical," although this group of believers has nothing to do with American Evangelicalism political activism or theology). As they do around the world, Roman Catholic churches in Germany recognized the spiritual authority of the Pope. Individual churches belong to parishes (*Gemeinden*), which are part of dioceses and archdioceses.

Evangelisch congregations belong to state church associations, some of which follow borders of states dating back to the Second German Empire. These associations are part of a national body called the Evangelische Kirche in Deutschland, or EKD. The *Evangelisch* church was created in the early 1800s as a forced union of what were then the two largest Protestant groups, the Lutherans and the Reformed. Both of these groups were created during the Protestant Reformation of the 1500s and were the established churches in various German states at various times. As a result, it's likely that German churches that are now *Evangelisch* will be referred to as Lutheran (*Lutherisch*) or Reformed (*Reformiert*) in historical records. In addition, a given village might have had both a Reformed and Lutheran congregation, resulting in two sets of concurrent registers being kept. However, a small minority of congregations resisted the merger and are known as "Old Lutherans."

A few other Protestant minority groups existed, such as Mennonites, the Amish, members of the Church of the Brethren, and Moravians. But because the only state churches endorsed by the various rulers were Catholic, Lutheran, or Reformed, most of these smaller groups headed for America, which is where the Germans became part of that aforementioned kaleidoscope.

While most Germans came to America as either mainstream Protestant (Lutheran or Reformed in Colonial times, Protestant later) or Catholic, the seeds of sectarian minority groups reached full flower when Germans settled in areas that stayed overwhelmingly German. This resulted in immigrants joining other Protestant denominations: Presbyterians, Methodists, and Episcopalians.

In Germany, church registers may be in either the original church or religious archives; many have been microfilmed and now digitized, and these will be profiled in chapters on the major genealogy websites as well as chapter 10. In America, where ethnic Germans adhered to a variety of different faiths, the information covered by surviving religious records (if you can find them) vary greatly. You'll find information on digitized American church records on major genealogy websites within those websites' respective chapters.

TOP GERMAN GENEALOGY METHODOLOGIES AND CAVEATS

While we've looked at general genealogy principles and some background information on German history and culture, we've yet to put the two together. While German genealogy shares research basics with other ethnic groups, some circumstances set German research apart and will add complications to your work. This section introduces some key steps involved in German genealogy; the methodologies and caveats outlined here are covered in more detail in *The Family Tree German Genealogy Guide* (Family Tree Books, 2014) <www.shopfamilytree.com/the-family-tree-german-genealogy-guide-u4833>.

Remember: Germany Is Not America

Many researchers mistakenly assume that the same strategies you use and records you look for when researching ancestors in America also apply to the Old World, but this isn't always the case. Because modern Germany developed differently from the United States, you'll have to challenge certain assumptions about genealogy research if you want to be successful. For example, you likely won't find the German tombstones of your relatives (a great resource for stateside researchers), as limited burial space forced religious institutions in Germany to reuse burial plots and remove memorial stones. Some more key things to consider when comparing US and German research are detailed below.

HISTORY OF DECENTRALIZATION

I'll point out several times in several ways that if your major goal is getting your German immigrant ancestor across the Atlantic, you need to know the name of the village of origin, called the *Heimat* ("home" or "motherland") in German. That's because Germany has a history of decentralization. As detailed earlier in this chapter, throughout the Middle Ages and into early modern times, German-speaking areas consisted of many small states—more than a thousand for a good chunk of history!—that at times bore only a passing allegiance to what was called the "Holy Roman Empire of the German Nation." Villages were often bought and sold or inherited by different minor dynasties as others went extinct. The Second German Empire (1871–1918) was the first state resembling Germany as we think of it today, even though it was technically a federal union consisting of a couple dozen states (with Prussia dominating as by far the largest).

As a result, Germany has no truly "national" archives and lacks a broad, uniformly kept federal record group like the US census (indeed, only a few individual German state censuses have been preserved with genealogically useful information). As a researcher, you must also keep track of which noble jurisdiction ruled a particular village during the time period you're researching, because this may have an impact on what archives have custody of the records you need.

CHANGING BORDERS

While the American story of Manifest Destiny was of a nation that expanded its boundaries and tamed a frontier, Germany's narrative has been one of expansion and then contraction as a result of losing both world wars in the twentieth century. Among the crucial factors to affect this narrative are a history of disunity mentioned earlier, the many German-speaking enclaves that formed from the Middle Ages onward throughout eastern Europe, and the growth of the Prussian state in the eighteenth and nineteenth centuries. The upshot is that there's a good chance one or more of your German ancestors comes from an area outside of today's Germany—and might be outside of any configuration of Germany ever. As part of tackling place names in chapter 3, we'll give you some online resources for dealing with these challenges.

Identify the Immigrant Ancestor

The immigration generation is a teeter-totter of sorts. For a majority of individuals, emigration from Germany to America was a one-way ticket that resulted in records only in Europe before immigration and only in America after. And since those American records may be more accessible to you in many cases, your first task is trying to find every such document directly about (or mentioning) the ancestor you believe to be an immigrant.

Among the most the common records to show either a village of origin or at least a particular German state are

- naturalizations (both the declarations of intent, known as "first papers," and petitions for naturalization, often called "final papers")
- baptisms of the immigrant's children
- marriage records
- church burial records
- tombstones
- obituaries
- US censuses
- family Bibles and registers
- fraternal societies' records
- military records such as enlistment and discharge papers and pension documents
- letters from relatives (and even their postmarks)

Looking for pieces of information such as occupations or unusual given names that might distinguish your immigrant will help you along the way. You also may need to use what eminent genealogist Elizabeth Shown Mills calls the FAN club of "friends, associates, and neighbors" as proxies in your research. Since so many Germans came as part of *clusters* (several families from the same village on a particular ship) or *chains* (people from the same village following each other over a span of years), identifying who your ancestors associated with in America—then researching those associates to find their origins—may lead to the same village.

Learn Language Skills

A lot of the records you will encounter—in both America and Germany—are written in the German language, but don't let this defeat you. Many online transcription and translation aids will be detailed in chapters 2 and 3. Right now, you just need to be prepared for the fact that you won't always be spoon-fed records in your native language. (Unless that language is German, of course.)

One word you'll need to know is *Rufnamen*. If you're just starting out—especially if you're looking at a lot of records that have been translated some time ago—you're going to think, "My, there are an awful lot of men named John." This is because most areas of Germany used a double naming (and, in the nineteenth century, sometimes a triple naming) system in which the individual was baptized with two or three given names but then was called by only one (hence the word *Rufname*, literally "call name"; plural: *Rufnamen*).

Until the 1800s, the first name Johann or Hans was given to virtually all German boys, and Anna or Maria to girls. Each person's middle name was the *Rufname*. In the nineteenth century, it become more complicated because children were often given three names and may use any of three as their *Rufname* in records.

FRAMING THE QUESTIONS

So, armed now with more knowledge about what you'll need as a German genealogist, we come back to what was mentioned in passing: the importance of framing your questions. You need goals—which some call a "research plan"—in order to formulate those questions. As Dave McDonald, author of the *Thinking Genealogically* blog **<onwresearch. thinkinggenealogically.com>** has written, family historians should ask, "What do I want to learn, and about whom or what?"

Framing a question too generally will likely result in blundering around the Internet, and that can also waste a lot of your time going down proverbial rabbit holes that don't yield genealogically useful information. On the other hand, framing a question too specifically may produce no results, and data may go by the wayside. This book is designed to give you appropriate focus in your website searches—running you through the most effective ways to use the Internet for German genealogy.

- Learn genealogy's basics before heading to the Internet for research. In particular, be aware that how you frame research questions will affect your results.

- Research the political and religious history of your ancestral villages to trace all records about them.

- Examine distinctive German methodologies (such as naming conventions and historical and cultural differences between Germany and the United States) to help you get the most out of your research time.

FRAMING THE QUESTION WORKSHEET

Getting the right answers is all about asking the right questions, what we've called "framing" questions in this chapter. To make the most of your time (and get the most out of your work), ask yourself the following questions before you begin a research session. You can download a Word-document version of this worksheet at <**ftu.familytreemagazine.com/ trace-your-german-roots-online**>.

1. What am I trying to accomplish?
The best genealogy research is methodical and goal oriented to maximize research time.

> *EXAMPLE: Rather than simply browsing Ancestry.com for your surname, you want to find your immigrant ancestor. Family legend states that he came from your maternal grandmother's side.*

My objective

_____

_____

2. What do I *really* know about my ancestor?
What pieces of information (date or place of birth/marriage/death, names of children, maiden name, etc.) are you missing? Remember your basic genealogy concepts—namely, go from the known to the unknown—and put them into practice by critically examining what information you have about that ancestor or ancestors.

> *EXAMPLE: You "know" when your maternal grandmother died because you've never forgotten that date—but you should get a copy of her death certificate anyway, because that way the date is not subject to memory's tricks. Plus, the death certificate may have additional information about her that you never knew or don't recall.*

Known facts related to my research goal

_____

_____

_____

3. What's my next step?

What does your current knowledge of ancestors tell you about the generation before? What can you learn about these ancestors, and what resources do you need to find to do so?

EXAMPLE: Your grandmother's death certificate lists her parents' names along with their states of birth. Your next step will likely be finding their birth information: Were there birth certificates in that state during the time period they were likely born? If not, what other sorts of records might exist that would give birth information, such as baptisms or newspaper listings or their tombstones?

My next steps

_____

_____

_____

During each step of the research process, revisit your questions and assumptions, reacting to what you find (or don't find) as a result of research on those questions. Then reformulate your questions.

2

RESEARCHING GERMAN GENEALOGY ON THE INTERNET

German genealogy and finding your way around German genealogy Internet resources can seem mighty simple to some people. I'm reminded of the time at a national conference when two women came up to the *German Life* magazine exhibit booth while notable (and now, unfortunately, late) Germanic genealogy scholar John T. Humphrey was present. The women apparently recognized neither John nor me and just started talking to each other about "how simple" German genealogy is. "All I did was write to the pastor and he sent me everything!" one babbled to the other. John and I looked at each other after they left, and he uttered, "So what have I spent the last half of my life doing German genealogy for? All I needed to do was write to the pastor."

Here's your tip of all tips: Yes, lightning can strike and you may get lucky. And as I said, many, many German genealogy resources are available to you. But to find them effectively and analyze them well takes some skill and likely more effort than just writing a letter to get "everything." What you need are ways to get around language barriers, some knowledge of political divisions and church groups, and some schooling about collaborative family trees. This chapter will give you all that and more, including a preview of the step-by-step tools you'll see in the rest of the book as well as an honest look at what you can and can't achieve on the Internet.

GETTING AROUND LANGUAGE BARRIERS

In terms of language and the language skills needed to use them effectively, websites for German genealogy will essentially fit into one of three categories:

1. Many sites (mostly those based in the United States) will be written in English.
2. Others will be written in German and require you to provide your own translation using one of a variety of translation services.
3. Some websites written in German will also offer an English version of the site.

When combined with the fact that many of the records you will be accessing are hand-written or printed in the German language, this potential linguistic roadblock is a call for a skills intervention—improving your German language skills or your skill at finding resources to help translate for you. You'll also need some knowledge of German phonetics and dialect, but we'll go over how to further arm yourself with those in chapter 3. For now, we're dealing with what to do when you're confronted with having to translate a German website.

Google Translate

As the makeup and functionality of the Internet has morphed and played a larger role in everyday life, looking for exactly what you want on the Web spawned the need for a search engine to separate the wheat from the chaff of the world's virtually assembled knowledge. Enter Google **<www.google.com>**, the greatest search engine known to man.

Merely searching for keywords on Google is valuable for anyone, including genealogists, but there's much more than that on the site. German genealogists can use Google for translations in two separate ways. First, Google's Translate feature **<translate.google.com>** lets you take a word, phrase, or passage and have it translated, quite roughly, from German to English (or between any of the hundreds of languages available).

Image **A** shows the screen you'll use to initiate translation. You may have to play with the click-on boxes below the word Translate, including one marked Detect language to switch the default language fields to what you wish.

> **POWER-USER TIP**
>
> **Double-check Translation Sources**
> When a German website has an easy-to-click button for an English-language version, be sure to give a visual double-check on whether the English version is a translation of the German site or a just a summary. If the latter, you may want to do your own translation using the step-by-step instructions in this chapter.

Google Translate is the most popular language translation tool on the Internet.

Another way you can use Google's translation features is to help you with that second category of German-language websites that does not supply an English-language version.

STEP-BY-STEP EXAMPLE: USING GOOGLE TO TRANSLATE A WEB PAGE

1 Copy the URL of the website you want to translate. Take, for example, the municipal website for the village of Grünstadt in Rheinland-Pfalz **<www.gruenstadt.de>**. This is a medium-size community, and the site has no English translation built in. To copy, highlight the URL in the browser bar and press control-C on a Windows PC or command-C on a Mac.

2 Paste that URL into the search box on Google **<www.google.com>** by pressing control-V on a Windows PC or command-V on a Mac, and clicking the magnifying glass or hitting the Enter key. Click on Translate this page.

3 A translated version of the page will load. Note that Google Translate will sometimes translate German names literally (*Grünstadt* is rendered here as "green city") and will not translate other text at all.

Online Dictionaries and Apps

As noted, Google Translate gives translations that are rough at times and fail to account for many contexts. Here are some other translation websites to consider as alternates and supplements (with assessments in part based on information from professional genealogist and linguist Glen W. Covert):

- BabelFish **<www.babelfish.com>**: It's better at detecting context than Google Translate, but you can't translate whole websites at once.

- BEOLINGUS—Your Online Dictionary **<dict.tu-chemnitz.de>**: This dictionary gives lots of results, including less formal translations that include street slang, idioms, and colloquialisms.

- Dict.cc Deutsch-Englisch Wörterbuch **<www.dict.cc>**: The strength of this particular translator is terminology specific to businesses and industry.

- LEO **<www.dict.leo.org>**: This online dictionary gives fewer results than Beolingus because it concentrates on more formal meanings.

- Linguee English-German Dictionary **<www.linguee.com>**: This excellent dictionary and translator gives a variety of sentences using the word or words in context, though, of course, it won't find every context.

Dictionaries with Archaic Words

As genealogists we're forever dealing with the archaic. That's the job description, after all: to trace the human form of antiques! For that reason, it sometimes helps to have a dictionary of archaic words. The best one of these that's been put online is Grimms' *Deutsches Wörterbuch* (German Dictionary) **<www.woerterbuchnetz.de/DWB>**—and yes, it's compiled by the same Brothers Grimm who gave us the collections of fairy tales. Because this is a work in the German language, you'll need to employ other translation tools, but the payoff is that many words no longer in use (but that show up in historic documents) will show up in Grimms'.

B

The University of Trier's website contains references that can help you decode German words that are no longer in use.

At the bottom of the Wörterbuchnetz home page <www.woerterbuchnetz.de> (image **B**), you'll find a number of additional old dictionaries and reference books on the University of Trier's website. These range from dialect dictionaries to Middle High German reference guides to a German law dictionary.

Resources for Learning German

We've been concentrating on using websites that do the heavy lifting for you, but as you saw with the old Grimms' dictionary, not all tools are going to spoon-feed you what you need to know. The following apps, podcasts, articles, courses, and sites are designed to help you learn more of the German language:

- Deutsche Welle <www.dw.de/learn-german/s-2469>, free online course as well as a free podcast called the Audiotrainer <www.dw.de/learn-german/audiotrainer/s-9677>
- Duolingo <www.duolingo.com>, free iOS and Android app
- Language Surfer: How to Pass the German A1 Test <www.languagesurfer.com/2013/08/19/how-to-pass-the-german-a1-test>, free website
- Learn German by Podcast <www.learngermanbypodcast.com>, free podcast
- Mango Languages <www.mangolanguages.com>, free iOS and Android app
- MindSnacks <www.mindsnacks.com>, $4.99 iOS app
- National Institute for Genealogical Studies <www.genealogicalstudies.com>, $89 online course
- Slow German <www.slowgerman.com/category/absolute-beginner>, free podcast
- SurvivalPhrases.com: German <www.survivalphrases.com/german>, free website

Printed Fraktur Font and Handwritten Script

Of course, even if you have the most fluent German language skills, German genealogy records can throw you a few more curveballs—here comes that archaic thing again! Before the 1940s, most printed German records used a Fraktur font, and handwritten documents

POWER-USER TIP

Check for Free First
Due to agreements between major websites, many German record databases are available in multiple places. Always check free sites first to see if they have what you need—you may discover the same data that pay sites such as Ancestry.com <www.ancestry.com> and MyHeritage <www.myheritage.com> require a subscription to access.

It's Not Easy—But It's Necessary

While you don't need a lot of German to succeed with German Internet research, the more language skills you can develop, the better able you will be to function on your own and with less help from German speakers. This is important because many records in America relating to your German ancestors—including some documents from generations after immigration, depending on the type of community in which your ancestors settled—will still be written in German. The sites listed here should give you some assistance, but as with many computer tools, they're often not nimble enough to account for dialects and spelling variants. For that, you'll need some knowledge of German phonetics (coming in chapter 3) to avoid problems such as faulty indexed transcriptions of records.

were composed in cursive scripts that may well appear to be chicken scratches to the naked eye. If you're going to make a serious attempt at finding the actual records and understanding them, you'll need to learn to "cut through the code" of these impediments. Here are a variety of online tools that can help:

- About.com: Old German Script—Kurrent **<www.genealogy.about.com/od/paleography/ig/old_handwriting/Kurrent.htm>**
- Brigham Young University: The German Script Tutorial **<script.byu.edu/Pages/German/en/welcome.aspx>**
- Family History Library Handwriting Guide: German Gothic **<feefhs.org/guides/German_Gothic.pdf>**
- Genealoger: German Genealogy—Language, Handwriting, and Script **<www.genealoger.com/german/ger_german_language.htm>**
- My Ancestors and Me: Helps for Translating That Old German Handwriting **<www.nancysfamilyhistoryblog.blogspot.com/2011/06/helps-for-translating-that-old-german.html>**
- Omniglot: German **<www.omniglot.com/writing/german.htm>**
- Suetterlin Schrift: German handwriting **<www.suetterlinschrift.de/Englisch/Sutterlin.htm>**

COLLABORATIVE TREES: PROS AND CONS

Putting together collaborative family trees on genealogy websites has moved from being one of the hottest things going just a few years ago to a much-debated paradigm among family historians. There's no doubt that these "pedigree databases" can produce potential research leads and jackpot moments of discovery. In fact, we'll discuss the three largest genealogy entities offering user-submitted family tree databases (FamilySearch.org, Ancestry.com, and MyHeritage) in part 2.

But there's also no doubt that in many cases, the public family trees that people post online are a huge echo chamber of unverified information. Does this mean you shouldn't use them for clues and forming hypotheses? Absolutely not. But does this mean that we should blithely add the ancestors found on someone's tree without checking whether the information about those ancestors is supported by evidence? Even more emphatically—absolutely not! Fact-checking and having a level of scrutiny are vital when evaluating others' family trees for your own research.

You also need to be prepared for a dose of disappointment if you attempt to contact the submitters of public family trees. Collaborative family trees on the major genealogy websites can be set with all manner of privacy levels; for example, fairly typical restrictions protect the information of living persons or limit access to only certain authorized people. And for many people today, genealogy is a passing fad. They put together what I have termed "carpenter trees." That is, they find one "board," perhaps a birth record, somewhere on the Internet (probably on some other online tree) and "nail" it along with another "board" (say a marriage record, found somewhere else on the Internet) of a similarly named person. When you ask them to share their sources, often these "carpenter genealogists" either don't reply at all or respond off point (often by asking you for more information about your family, presumably so they can keep their "nailing" process going). The net result is often finding out that the promising new lead is just another voice bouncing around in that echo chamber.

Still, don't dismiss these collaborative trees without investigation. You can occasionally make new research acquaintances. You may also find references to actual records that will put you on the right track—especially if it's a case where an ancestor moved to an unexpected place or did something else that your research methodology wouldn't have picked up. But remember that even if what you find is a completely unsourced name, date, or place that was previously unknown to you—well, you can formulate new questions or a new hypothesis and set out to find documentation of said name, date, or place. No clue should be shunned.

Finally, these public family trees are not the only source of collaboration. You'll

POWER-USER TIP

Be Sure to See It All

Be wary when looking at any website with digitized records to decide whether you've seen "all" records of a category, for two reasons. First, most records on the Web were produced by microfilm-to-digital transfer, so if an original record page went unmicrofilmed, it will also be an undigitized page. Second, large websites often have databases will all-inclusive titles (think "German Births, 1558–1898") but are hard to drill down as far as which selected records they actually include.

discover that some German genealogy-themed social media sites are worth your attention. We'll talk about these in chapter 13.

WHAT YOU CAN AND CAN'T ACCOMPLISH

We've now armed you with some methodologies and given you the tools to investigate the three types of websites in terms of language. As we explore the big sites in part 2 and specialty sites in part 3, you'll see that you might well be able to accomplish your German research goals without darkening the door of a library or archives. This would have been impossible just a few years ago.

But while complete online research is *possible* today, it's likely that you will need to go "on the ground" for additional assistance. This is particularly true if your ancestry is from a more "backward" area of Germany, but it can also happen if you need to do special analysis to find the right records.

For example, a genealogist could learn the Rhineland hometown of her ancestor from an American church record but have difficulty finding more information on it solely from the Internet. A series of (printed) books on the boundaries of the church parishes indicates that the hometown would be in a particular parish, which no doubt it was for the time period that the author used. But that was not the time period the genealogist's ancestor was in the hometown. The researcher then has to map out that entire Rhineland area and actually view several area parishes' records from the time period to determine which one was the correct hometown for her ancestor, and many towns' records have still not been digitized.

There will be a day when all these records, maps, and microfilms will be digitized, but that day is not upon us yet. But still, many, many genealogical questions and problems can be solved with the right Internet searches.

KEYS TO SUCCESS

- Leverage the capabilities of Google Translate and online German dictionaries to help you translate German sites and archaic words and phrases. Be sure to check for English versions of German sites.

- Become familiar with the German language as well as the printed font and handwritten script in which older documents were written.

- Examine collaborative trees carefully, as they can be both an echo chamber of bad information and a way to trade information or gain valuable clues.

- Develop realistic expectations about what you can accomplish online. Some German research problems will be beyond the scope of any website and require on-site analysis.

3

UNTANGLING GERMAN PLACE NAMES AND SURNAMES

The German language can be tricky for non-native speakers, and it's easy for words to become lost in translation. This was the case when I was trying to visit an ancestor's hometown. When I began my genealogical searching some three decades ago, a single, solitary *Heimat* of my ancestors had been handed down to me: the tiny village of Elsoff in the former *Grafschaft* (countship) of Wittgenstein, now part of the German *Land* Nordrhein-Westfalen. As such, making a pilgrimage of sorts to Elsoff became a goal of mine. During my first two trips to Germany, I didn't have the moxie to go to this region myself. So I queried two friends, the German couple hosting me, about going there, only to be told that it was too far to travel. From merely looking at the map, I knew this wasn't true. But not wanting to be the stereotypical "ugly American," I didn't press the issue.

Finally, I wrote about wanting to visit the town in an e-mail to the couple after my first two visits. Seeing the name in print must have made up for my apparently barbarous German accent, because the hostess told me that when I visited and was speaking about the town, she thought I said *Elsass*, the German name for Alsace, when I was actually trying to say *Elsoff*. Alsace, an area that is now part of France but once was an ethnic German area, would have indeed been quite a distance from my hosts' home an hour north of

Frankfurt am Main. I visited Elsoff on my next trip across the Atlantic. No better evidence than this has shown me how easily German names can be verbally garbled.

We've already primed you with some terminology, translation helps, and historical background in chapters 1 and 2. In this chapter, we'll cover tools needed for "ungarbling" the names of your ancestors and the places associated with them so you'll be ready to tackle the websites profiled in parts 2 and 3. Some of these helpful resources deal with German names and phonetics, while others offer map and gazetteer resources and additional German historical background. The worksheet at the end of this chapter will also be a helpful guide for putting together all possible spelling variants for place and surnames.

PRIMER ON GERMAN PHONETICS

A truism of genealogy is that only a foolish person immediately says "But my ancestor's name wasn't spelled that way" when confronted with a record that uses a different spelling than the one the researcher is accustomed to. When you add the complexity of the many dialects of German used in Europe and the fact that many American records were created by an English-speaking clerk, enumerator, or tax collector trying to figure out what a semi-literate German-speaking immigrant was trying to tell him—well, that's a recipe for a smorgasbord of place and surname spellings in the records you'll find.

The short course in German phonetics—there's a longer course in chapter 6 of *The Family Tree German Genealogy Guide* and more details in websites that we'll profile shortly—is that several consonants frequently are interchangeable. These consonants are the *b* and *p*; *d* and *t* and *th*; *g* and *k* and *c*; and (because of pronunciation differences) the German *w* and the English *v*. For vowels, the number one source of confusion is that the German language has vowels with *Umlaute* (umlauts), generally written as a pair of dots over the *a*, *o*, *u*, and *y* (the last usually appearing only in the Swiss German dialect) that affect the pronunciation of the vowel. The use of umlauts is a shortcut for putting an *e* after the previous vowel. Another German-language peculiarity is that a "double s" is frequently represented as an "S-zet" (*ß*) that is rendered much like (and therefore frequently mistaken for) a Roman script uppercase *B*.

Whenever you encounter a new German surname in your genealogy, you should think about that surname not in terms of *the* spelling but rather as a set of spelling variants, using phonetics to flesh out the universe of possibilities for the name. While given names also involve spelling variants, you'll likely be able to identify the individuals correctly if you remember the *Rufname* concept from chapter 1. You must also understand that many German nicknames are used in records but the Germans often chop off the first syllable in forming diminutives—think *Stina* for "Christina" and *Klaus* for "Nicklaus."

The same goes for new place names, especially if you don't immediately find them on a map (or are unsure whether you've indeed found the right town—for example, maybe the area of Germany doesn't fit other information you have). Use the *phonetischen Namen Karte* (phonetic name chart) at the end of this chapter to come up with lists of spelling variants so you are attuned to all possibilities when searching databases for records or browsing through documents. Another resource that will be profiled in the chapter on MyHeritage <www.myheritage.com> is the site's "Global Name Translation."

Understanding German Phoentics

For a quick-and-dirty recap of how different letters are pronounced in German, use About.com's German Language Web page on The German Phonetic Spelling Code <www.german.about.com/library/blfunkabc.htm>. While this is primarily a code used for spelling out letters for use in broadcasts, it gives the basic sounds that will help you with German in general, too.

A much more sophisticated online look at German phonetics is part of the University of Portsmouth in England's Paul Joyce German Course. Joyce's A Guide to German Pronunciation <www.joycep.myweb.port.ac.uk/pronounce> (image **A**) details what you'll need to come up with the most likely pronunciations of various German names. Joyce's guide illustrates pronunciation rules in depth, covering every German letter as well as combinations of letters.

Finding German Surnames in Germany

In addition to testing out phonetic variants of surnames, some Internet databases allow you to get an idea of where those surnames are found in today's Germany. While there's no guarantee that the highest concentrations of a surname in modern Germany will be an exact match of those historical concentrations, these databases do give you a starting point for geographic hypotheses on your family origins if other records have not borne fruit. The data from both the websites profiled below come from German telephone

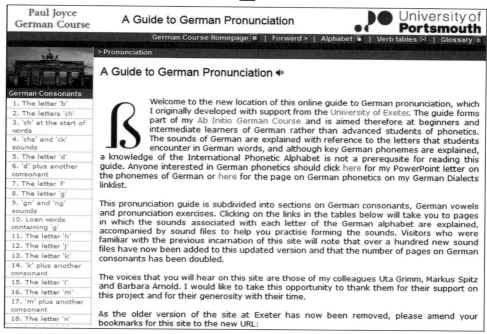

Paul Joyce
German Course

A Guide to German Pronunciation

University of **Portsmouth**

German Course Homepage | Forward > | Alphabet | Verb tables | Glossary

> Pronunciation

A Guide to German Pronunciation ◄»

Welcome to the new location of this online guide to German pronunciation, which I originally developed with support from the University of Exeter. The guide forms part of my Ab Initio German Course and is aimed therefore at beginners and intermediate learners of German rather than advanced students of phonetics. The sounds of German are explained with reference to the letters that students encounter in German words, and although key German phonemes are explained, a knowledge of the International Phonetic Alphabet is not a prerequisite for reading this guide. Anyone interested in German phonetics should click here for my PowerPoint letter on the phonemes of German or here for the page on German phonetics on my German Dialects linklist.

This pronunciation guide is subdivided into sections on German consonants, German vowels and pronunciation exercises. Clicking on the links in the tables below will take you to pages in which the sounds associated with each letter of the German alphabet are explained, accompanied by sound files to help you practise forming the sounds. Visitors who were familiar with the previous incarnation of this site will note that over a hundred new sound files have now been added to this updated version and that the number of pages on German consonants has been doubled.

The voices that you will hear on this site are those of my colleagues Uta Grimm, Markus Spitz and Barbara Arnold. I would like to take this opportunity to thank them for their support on this project and for their generosity with their time.

As the older version of the site at Exeter has now been removed, please amend your bookmarks for this site to the new URL:

German Consonants

1. The letter 'b'
2. The letters 'ch'
3. 'ch' at the start of words
4. 'chs' and 'ck' sounds
5. The letter 'd'
6. 'd' plus another consonant
7. The letter 'f'
8. The letter 'g'
9. 'gn' and 'ng' sounds
10. Loan words containing 'g'
11. The letter 'h'
12. The letter 'j'
13. The letter 'k'
14. 'k' plus another consonant
15. The letter 'l'
16. The letter 'm'
17. 'm' plus another consonant
18. The letter 'n'

Paul Joyce's website guides you through how every German letter can combine with the others and how letters and these combinations are pronounced.

books; in chapter 11, we'll also show you how to conduct searches for individuals and businesses on a website with the all-Germany telephone directory.

Another website is Ken McCrea's GermanNames **<www.germannames.com>**, which charges nominal fees for maps and German postal code listings of surnames. A book of the surname maps of the five hundred most frequent surnames is also available from the same author.

The Geogen Surname Mapping site **<legacy.stoepel.net>** will generate three types of data on surnames:

- a "relative distribution" that gives the number of instances of the surname per million entries in the phone book, which adjusts for the potential of a lot of instances of a surname purely because of an area's population

- an "absolute distribution," which puts the actual numbers of entries into groups

- a pie chart showing the percentages in which the surname is found in current German states

Next, let's take a closer look at how the site works.

STEP-BY-STEP EXAMPLE: MAPPING WITH GEOGEN

1 Call up the Geogen website **<legacy.stoepel.net>**. Note: The site may not work in all Web browsers. If you have difficulty loading the site, try another browser. Type the surname of interest into the box. For this example, I'll use the surname *Rathmacher*.

2 Click on the links in the Surname Map tab to generate the maps and pie chart. The Community tab shows notes left by other searchers, if any.

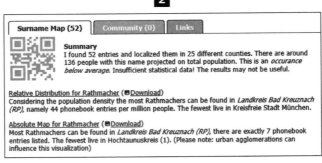

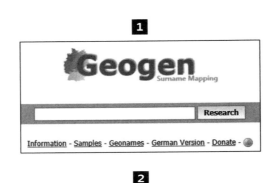

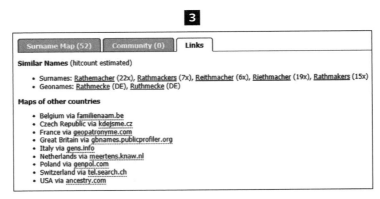

3 Select the Links tab to see a number of potential spelling variants and the number of entries for each. In addition, this tab offers maps of the surname in other European countries and the United States as well as other Web links.

BEST ONLINE GERMAN MAP RESOURCES

Because of the many changes to political divisions in German lands, you must always think about the *Heimat* not only in terms of the "now of now" but also the "now of then"—with "then" possibly referring to multiple time periods. While you'll learn more about this in chapter 9, a number of websites will help you bridge this gap between today and yesterday, hopefully leaving no town unfound. Some have actual maps; others are gazetteers (essentially, place-name encyclopedias).

Two of best tools are *Meyers Gazetteer of the German Empire* on Ancestry.com **<search.ancestry.com/search/db.aspx?dbid=1074>** and the GOV *Historic Gazetteer* on Genealogy.net **<gov.genealogy.net/search/index>**), which will both be explored in depth in part 2. Here we'll discuss some of the smaller resources that can help you unravel German place names and locate them in modern Germany.

Maps

As far as historical maps go, none are more detailed or more accessible than the *Atlas des Deutschen Reichs* (Atlas of the German Kingdom) by Ludwig Ravenstein (1883). This fully searchable map was digitized by the University of Wisconsin and is available for searching at **<uwdc.library.wisc.edu/collections/German/Ravenstein>**. Once you find a village in Ravenstein's atlas, you can compare the area to a modern-day map.

Another noteworthy source of historical maps is *The Family Tree Historical Maps Book: Europe* (Family Tree Books, 2015), which has an index to the online source for each of the maps contained in the work, allowing readers to blow up each map to any size they wish. You can learn more about this resource at **<www.shopfamilytree.com/family-tree-historical-maps-book-europe>**.

For maps of modern Germany, you can try using Google Maps **<maps.google.com>**, although you'll only see one match for each village name you search, even if that name applies to multiple towns. Instead, the engine will find one village with the entered name while ignoring the others, which can be frustrating. A workaround is to search for neighboring villages instead, if you know any. The German National Tourist Board **<www.germany.travel/en/index.html>** has a variety of maps among its arsenal of resources. But the best online, modern-day maps are served up by the folks from ViaMichelin **<www.viamichelin.com>**.

1

2

Perform a Full-Text Phrase Search by Title, Subcollection, or Journals and Series

To perform a Boolean or proximity search or to browse the collection, choose one of these links:
Boolean Search | Proximity Search | Browse

Search the full text of some or all items in this collection.*

Entire work ∨
Search within a specific title:
All ∨

Search | Clear

3

Ravenstein, Ludwig *Atlas des Deutschen Reichs : bearb. von Ludwig Ravenstein* (1883)

Namen-Register zur Spezialkarte des deutschen Reichs, pp. i-xxx

Page xxiii (1 match)
Page xxv (1 match)

STEP-BY-STEP EXAMPLE: USING RAVENSTEIN'S ATLAS

1 Go to the home page for the atlas on the University of Wisconsin's site **<uwdc.library. wisc.edu/collections/German/Ravenstein>**. You'll likely want to begin using the atlas by keyword searching—click Search the full text. To begin browsing the atlas, skip to step 5.

2 In the search box, enter the name of the village. The default will search for all titles included in the University's German Studies Collection, but you can narrow your search to a specific title, such as Ravenstein's atlas.

3 View your results, which are organized by title. I entered *Sprendlingen* and received two entries from Ravenstein's atlas.

4

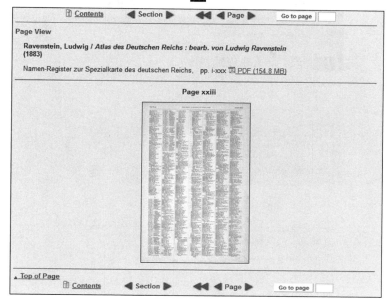

5

4 Access the pages from the PDF at the top of the results page.

5 If you can't find information on your town (or you want to manually browse the atlas' pages), return to the atlas' home page and click Browse the Atlas.

6 On the resulting browse page, choose one of the sections of the map.

7 Click the map portion's thumbnail to load a PDF of the section in your browser or right-click (PCs) or control-click (Macs) to download the file your desktop. You can also browse each section by page in your browser, though you'll likely want to view the section's PDF to see all of the section's pages on one screen.

8 View the map's PDF and zoom in and out as needed.

6

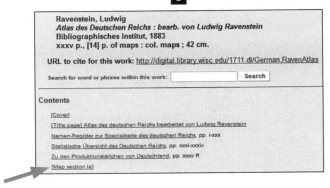

7

8

Gazetteers

We've already given you the "tease" about the mega-gazetteers that will be profiled in part 2 (and the big websites also have some regional gazetteers, too), but one stand-alone site deserves mention: Kartenmeister <www.kartenmeister.com>. This is a comprehensive database for villages in the former Prussian areas that now lie mostly in Poland.

STEP-BY-STEP EXAMPLE: SEARCHING FOR PLACE NAMES IN KARTENMEISTER

1 Go to the Kartenmeister home page <www.kartenmeister.com>.

2 Scroll to the bottom of page to find the search box and enter a term. In this example, we'll use *Niederung*.

3

There are 3 records that match your search criteria.

German Name	County/Kreis
Niederung	Schlochau
Niederung	Schlochau
Niederung	Schlochau

4

German Name	Niederung
Polish/Russian Name	Zdrojki
Kreis/County	Schlochau
German Province	Westpreussen
Today's Province	Pomorskie
Location	East 17°14' North 53°47'
Google Map	Google Maps (Niederung)
Map Number	25
Location Description	This village/town is located 1.2 km and 225 degrees from Prechlau, which is known today as Przechlewo
Lutheran Parish	Prechlau 1905
Catholic Parish	Prechlau 1905
Standesamt/Civil Registry	Prechlau 1905
Gemeindelexikon/Town Index	II-23-66
Population By Year/Einwohner	1905: 148

3 View your results. Kartenmeister returns three results for *Niederung*.

4 Click on a result to bring up a grid with information about the town. You'll learn that Niederung's Polish/Russian name is Zdrojki, that it was in the German province West-preussen, and that it was in the parish Prechlau.

ADDITIONAL HISTORICAL BACKGROUND

You've been given the "once over lightly" version of German history in chapter 1, but you'll often need to get deep into the weeds to determine which political units your ancestor's village of origin belonged to throughout time. In some instances, the historical maps in this chapter will help clarify things for you; in other cases, you'll need chapter 9's more detailed breakdown to get you to the right places for records about the village. In the meantime, you may want additional historical information on Germany, and several websites provide you with this sort of information. The best is German History in Documents and Images <www.germanhistorydocs.ghi-dc.org>, which describes itself as "a comprehensive collection of original historical materials documenting German history from the beginning of the early modern period to the present." Each section presents narrative as well as documents from the chronological period being studied, with full English translations.

Try, Try Again

Records (and record transcriptions) aren't foolproof, so you'll need to think outside the box when searching. Whether you're dealing with a website database that requires an exact name match or one that accounts for spelling variations in its search, you'll need to play with the spellings of personal names and place names to make sure you see all possible records. No search algorithm can successfully account for all possible differences.

NOW LET'S FIND SOME GERMAN ANCESTORS ON THE WEB!

Over the three chapters in this book's part 1, you've been exposed to basics of both genealogy in general and German genealogy in specific, resources to obtain the language skills you'll need for the various types of websites, and the tools for ungarbling names of places and people. You're probably now feeling like a race car driver waiting for the green flag to take off. Next, in part 2, you will see how big outfits such as Ancestry.com **<www.ancestry. com>**, FamilySearch.org **<www.familysearch.org>**, and MyHeritage **<www.myheritage.com>** serve information to you while the other mega-sites Genealogy.net **<compgen.de>** (the ultimate multifaceted help site) and Archion **<archion.de>** (the specialized Protestant church record spot) give you their scads of data. Then part 3 will start with the questions that come most to German genealogists' minds and match them up with the websites that have the best possibility of giving answers. *Damen und Herren*, start your engines!

KEYS TO SUCCESS

- Study German language and phonetics, as these will affect how a place or surname is spelled (and misspelled) in records.

- Identify geographic surname concentrations to help you form hypotheses about where your ancestors came from.

- Use online map resources (like maps and gazetteers) for both historical and modern Germany to pinpoint place names found in records.

PHONETISCHEN NAMEN KARTE (PNK) WORKSHEET

Centuries of mistranslated and misheard names have made tracking German place names and surnames into historical records difficult. However, you'll find that words had a tendency to be misspelled in different ways based on how non-German speakers may have misinterpreted them. This three-step PNK worksheet is designed to help you identify these potential spelling variations so you can broaden your search for your ancestors and their hometown. You can download a Word-document version of this worksheet at <**ftu.familytreemagazine. com/trace-your-german-roots-online**>.

1. Study phonetic hints. While you won't be able to predict all misspellings, you can trouble-shoot for the most common transcription mistakes.

Initial Letters	<ul><li>*H* may have been dropped</li><li>Names beginning with *Y* may have originally have begun with *J*</li><li>*V* names may have begun with a *W*</li></ul> *See Consonant Interchanges and Vowel Shifts for more.*
Vowel Shifts	Any umlauted vowel (i.e., any vowel with two dots over it) can shift into just about any other vowel in English records! In addition, the second letter in German vowel combinations is usually the one that "speaks"—e.g., *ie* is a long *e*, *ei* is a long *i*, and *eu* makes the *oy* sound. Many German "short" vowels are interchangeably re-spelled. "Long" vowels include shifts such as:<ul><li>*ei* or *ey* or *ai* or *ay*</li><li>*ie* or *i* or *ü*</li><li>*e* or *ee* or *ä*</li><li>*äu* or *eu*</li><li>*ü* or *y*</li></ul>
Consonant Interchanges	Letters that can be interchanged are:<ul><li>*b* or *v* or *f*</li><li>*d* or *t* or *th*</li><li>*f* or *pf* or *ff*</li><li>*k* or *c* or *g*</li><li>*s* or *z*</li></ul>
Combinations/Syllables	Combinations/syllables in original manuscripts may be today interpreted as:<ul><li>*sch* as *s* or *sh*</li><li>*-bach* as *-back* or *-baugh*</li><li>*-mann* as *-man*</li><li>*-ts* as *-tz* or *-z*</li><li>*-berg* or *-burg* as *-berk* or *-berck*</li><li>*-le* as *-ly* or *-ley*</li></ul>
Translations	Check for English versions of the German name (or its syllables) in case it was translated (e.g., check *Little* for *Klein*, *Baker* for *Bäcker*, and *Shoemaker* for *Schuhmacher*).

2. Create a master variant diagram. This chart, which you can fill in below, lists the surname as you know it today, possible vowel or consonant shifts that apply to the name, and each spelling variant you've identified by using the possible letter differences. Two examples have been provided for your reference.

Surname Today	Possible Vowel, Consonant, and Syllable Shifts	Possible Spelling Variants
Snyder	Sn or Shn or Schn y or ei or i d or t or th -er or -ur	Snider, Sniter, Snytur, Sneider, Sneiter, Sneither, Schnyder, Schnyter, Schnyther, Schneiter, Schneither, Shniter, Shneider, Shneiter
Zeifenbeck	z or s ei or ie or e or i or ü f or pf or ff en or in -beck or -baugh or -bach	Ziefenbach, Zeifenbaugh, Sieffenbach, Sieffenbaugh, Siephenbeck, Züffenbach, Süphenbach, Seifenbeck

3. Begin searching records for spelling variants. Be sure to record what search terms you use and in which databases you search, as this will save you from repeating your efforts.

PART TWO

TOP GERMAN GENEALOGY WEBSITES

4

FAMILYSEARCH.ORG: THE LARGEST FREE GENEALOGY WEBSITE

The landscape of genealogy research is changing. As someone who cut his teeth toward the end of genealogy's "Gutenberg age"—the era of books, paper records, and record keeping—I knew when the tipping point toward "digital first" was reached. I had returned from the Family History Library (FHL) in Salt Lake City, Utah (the crown jewel of the Church of Jesus Christ of Latter-day Saints' genealogy efforts), with several generations of new records for a client with ancestors in Württemberg.

Because the village of origin had been supplied by the client, I hadn't bothered to plug the immigrants' names into FamilySearch.org <www.familysearch.org>, the ever-growing digital arm of a genealogy project undertaken by the Church of Jesus Christ of Latter-day Saints (often simply called "the Church" in Utah and by its members). But when I did, I found that some of the information I had found by painstakingly searching microfilms of German church records was already in searchable databases on the FamilySearch site.

While genealogists who aren't Mormon might sometimes be blasé about or express a less-than-serious attitude towards some rites of the Church (such as offering baptism to deceased ancestors), the Mormon commitment to genealogy, founded on the principle of an eternal family, is worthy of respect and an undeniable boon to family history researchers.

Starting as the Genealogical Society of Utah and now branded as FamilySearch, the Church's efforts to preserve the ancestral history have ranged from funding a worldwide microfilm program beginning in the 1930s to heading extraction efforts that put hundreds of millions of names into the International Genealogical Index (first on microfiche in the 1973, then migrated to CD-ROMs in the 1980s). After decades of this work, the Church has created the world's top research repository in the FHL and is now digitizing that stock of more than two million microfilms (with searchable indexes) for its FamilySearch.org website. Each step of the way, the Latter-day Saints have been the leading source for German genealogy information, and today FamilySearch.org remains indispensable.

IT'S ALL FREE

It's said that FamilySearch.org is the world's number one free genealogy website, and this is the one of the few times that such a claim isn't an overstatement. FamilySearch.org is a veritable hydra of a site: Even when you've struck out with one resource, you'll have plenty more to choose from. A description of the site and its holdings is worthy of its own book—indeed, there is one: *Unofficial Guide to FamilySearch.org* by Dana McCullough (Family Tree Books, 2015), available at **<www.shopfamilytree.com/unofficial-guide-familysearch>**. This chapter is going to review a few basics about the site and dwell on the many features of interest to those doing German genealogy.

Because it's free, FamilySearch.org is a great place to start searching for your German ancestors. Whether using the databases, browsing through digitized records, looking at the FamilySearch Catalog to plan microfilm research, or using one of the many learning tools such as the FamilySearch Wiki, you can't go wrong with FamilySearch.org. You do not have to register to use the site, but you likely will want to do so to enable you to post trees as well as order as-of-yet-undigitized microfilms for viewing near you (more on that later).

FamilySearch.org's home page currently consists of four menus: Family Tree, Memories, Search, and Indexing. While all these options have items that may be useful to you, we'll be concentrating on the many uses of Search (image **A**), as well as mentioning Indexing and its implications for German genealogy researchers.

Hovering over Search will reveal more specific options (image **B**), each of which will be described in detail in this chapter:

- **Records:** You'll spend most of your time here, with FamilySearch.org's many databases to mine and images to browse. We'll run through how you can make best use of these prime assets later in this chapter.

- **Genealogies:** These are a number of pedigree-linked databases of varying accuracy, some of which have been around for decades and others that have been more recently contributed (and are likely better sourced).

A

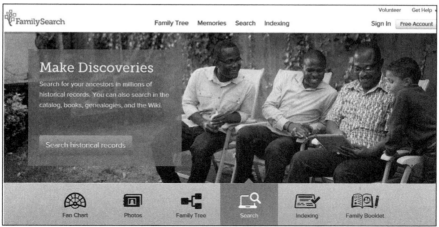

Begin your research on FamilySearch.org by seeing what resources are available for German researchers.

B

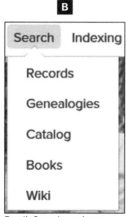

FamilySearch.org has a number of features you can use in research.

POWER-USER TIP

Look Before You Pay

As has been said earlier in this book, see what you can get for free before you pay for it. Many resources that you can access on paid websites can also be found on FamilySearch.org.

- **Catalog:** Here, you can search for all the materials that are part of the FamilySearch Catalog (once called the FHL Catalog, or FHLC) and learn how to access them.
- **Books:** The Family History Books digitization project can be accessed here.
- **Wiki:** This is the home of the Family History Research Wiki, FamilySearch's ever-expanding encyclopedia of articles relating to genealogy research.

Also remember that while FamilySearch is speedily marching toward full digitization, some of its FHL microfilm and book resources are restricted (e.g., owners or copyright holders of the resources in question) from giving users at-home digital access—or even from being digitized at all. Some archives only allow Church members to have remote access to the online records. Note that you may get a notice that online films are "temporarily unavailable" even though they're restricted films. Whenever you get such a notice, try asking FamilySearch Support whether the restriction is truly "temporary" (which would mean someone else is using the resource) or essentially permanent. You can still *learn* about such restricted resources on FamilySearch.org, and we'll show you what the best ways to gain offline access.

And whether they're restricted or not, a substantial portion of the microfilm (including many German church records) and book collections (including loads of tomes related to German genealogy: pedigrees, histories, record abstracts, and the like) is not yet digitized. That's another reason why we'll talk about using the Catalog on FamilySearch.org: to plan research if you go to Salt Lake City or order films to a local FamilySearch Center run by the Church.

PRIME ONLINE ASSETS

The two FamilySearch.org assets of widest interest are its collections of digitized and indexed records. While you might think of these two categories of resources as heading toward each other like speeding railcars that will come together in a spectacular explosion of genealogical records access—instead of a colossal train wreck!—for now they are on separate tracks and both worthy of the German genealogist's attention.

The thing to remember is that in many cases (at this point) the imaged collections are not indexed, and the indexed collections sometimes won't have images. Regardless of whether the collection is indexed, you'll want to access an image of the record because it likely has additional information and context that an index might not capture.

You can access both the digitized and indexed collections by going to the Search tab on the FamilySearch.org home page and clicking on Records, which yields a number of ways to access records on the site similar to the overall Search form (image **C**).

On the left-hand side (or on top, depending on the width of your computer screen) of the page, you'll see a search form titled Search Historical Records. This is your primary entryway to the indexed collections since, naturally, results from the images-only collections won't show here.

On the right-hand side (or the bottom depending on width) of the Records page is a map of the world titled Research by Location. If you click on the Europe map, a listing of countries comes up; choosing Germany will show you the collections, both indexed

C

FamilySearch.org's Search Historical Records page allows you to search for records by type, year, name, or country. You can also search in individual countries by selecting a region on the map of the world, then by clicking the name of an individual nation.

D

While not all of the microfilmed collections have been indexed, you can still browse through all of the published databases that have been digitized.

and image-only, that have German records. This leads to a page called Germany Indexed Historical Records that has a search form. You can search all the collections pertaining to Germany or drill down by choosing one particular database. At the bottom of the Germany research page is a listing of the image-only (unindexed) collections, which can be called up for individual browsing.

If you don't wish to limit yourself to the collections marked with the Germany title, you can also hit Browse All Published Collections under the maps of the world. The page that results (titled Historical Record Collections, image **D**) allows you to look at the names of the better than two thousand collections (more than fifty of which are strictly German records) or "Filter by collection name" and pick up collection titles relevant to your search that may not have Germany in the title. A camera icon appears when the collections have images as opposed to merely indexed records.

STEP-BY-STEP EXAMPLE: BEGINNING A SEARCH FOR RECORDS ON FAMILYSEARCH.ORG

1 From the Search page **<www.familysearch.org>**, click Europe (which includes all of Russia) on the world map.

2 Choose Germany from the scrolling list of nations that results.

3 B

Germany Image Only Historical Records

Can't find records for your ancestors when you search? Try our collections that haven't been indexed yet. Select a collection to start browsing the images.

* = Recently added or updated

Birth, Marriage, and Death	Images	Last Updated	
Germany, Anhalt, Dessau, City Directories, 1866-1919	8,605	12 Apr 2013	
Germany, Bavaria, Traunstein, Family Group Sheets, 1830-1900	54,076	22 Oct 2013	
Germany, Brandenburg, Bernau bei Berlin, Jewish Records, 1688-1872	2,058	05 Feb 2013	
Germany, Hesse, Civil Registration, 1874-1927	2,289,166	05 Dec 2012	
Germany, Hesse, Frankfurt, Civil Registration, 1811-1814, 1833-1928	386,801	10 Jul 2014	
Germany, Hesse-Nassau, Civil Registers and Church Books, 1701-1875	231,317	28 Nov 2012	
Germany, Hessen, Darmstadt City Records, 1627-1940	55,528	12 Oct 2012	
Germany, Prussia, Brandenburg, Heegermühle, Church Records, 1664-1824	520	24 Jan 2012	
Germany, Prussia, East Prussia, Königsberg, Index to Funeral Sermons and Memorials, 1700-1900	8,430	18 Apr 2012	
Germany, Prussia, Pomerania, Labes, Church Records, 1647-1764	639	10 Sep 2013	
Germany, Prussia, Pomerania, Stralsund, Church Book Indexes, 1600-1900	457,603	05 Dec 2012	
Germany, Prussia, Saxony, Halle, Miscellaneous City Records, 1401-1926	125,430	01 Nov 2012	
Germany, Prussia, Saxony, Various Protestant Church Records, 1594-1951	4,056	18 Jun 2014	
Germany, Rhineland-Palatinate Church Record Extractions and Family Registers, 1600-1925	106,564	12 Oct 2012	

3 Select which database you'd like to search. At the top is a search box for indexed records (image **3 A**) and the bottom has a list of the unindexed, image-only records (image **3 B**).

Indexed Collections

It stands to reason that if records of the vital events of birth, marriage, and death are a genealogist's big three resources, then those indexed collections of documents from Germany would be the largest. And so they are. About fifty million such records and their substitutes are kept in the FamilySearch.org indexed collections, under the following titles:

- Germany Births and Baptisms, 1558–1898
- Germany Deaths and Burials, 1582–1958
- Germany Marriages, 1558–1929

Each of these databases can be searched separately. And while they each contain millions of records, they are by no means a complete record of any of the three vital events between the dates noted; they represent the work of the FamilySearch Indexing volunteers.

We'll look at the Germany Births and Baptisms, 1558–1898, database as a step-by-step example. The following search fields are available (you can leave almost all of them blank, though you do need to fill in a surname):

- First Names
- Last Names
- Gender

- Birthplace
- Birth Year (Range): From and To boxes
- Search with a Relationship: a click box to fill in one or both parents' names
- Restrict Records By: ways of narrowing a search to look at records from a certain source (such as one particular microfilm)

The First Names, Last Names, and Birthplace boxes can be checkmarked to return only data that exactly matches the search criteria.

What's great about these collections is that the Citing This Collection information at the bottom gives you the exact FHL microfilm number from which the information came—see this chapter's section on the FamilySearch Catalog on deciphering this information. This will be helpful if you decide you want to see a microfilm copy of the original. In the case of this record, for instance, that's important because the original will have baptismal sponsors' names and seeing it in the context of the original might offer additional clues. For example, the baptism above this one may show the Heuschele parents were sponsors for someone else's child—and that someone else might be a relative. Or there may be a marginal notation in the original that will have an impact on your search (such as the death of the individual) that didn't fit into the pieces of data being captured during indexing.

You'd think that having access to such huge databases can't help but be good, right? Well, you'd be right and wrong. Yes, these databases are great first spots to check for your ancestors' respective vital events. But determining exactly what you've looked at when you do searches in these databases is an errand in imprecision. The closest you'll get are coverage tables in the FamilySearch Wiki that show the number of records from the respective German states.

Other indexed databases are substantially smaller than those offered by the "big three," but they can still be worth accessing depending on your geographic interest. Some also link to images of the records in question. Holdings include several databases of "church book duplicates," some civil registrations, census records from Mecklenburg-Schwerin, and a few collections of city and municipal records. A couple of substantial collections include church records from places such as Pomerania and Posen that are no longer part of Germany.

Databases of American records, of course, may be relevant to your German research, especially if you're still at the stage of discovering your ancestor's *Heimat*. Two collections with German in their titles are United States Germans to America Index, 1850–1897 (an incomplete indexing of Germans in the US passenger arrival lists), and United States, Obituaries, American Historical Society of Germans from Russia, 1899–2012 (more than four hundred thousand images and indexes of obituary records taken by the American Historical Society of Germans from Russia).

STEP-BY-STEP EXAMPLE: SEARCHING AN INDIVIDUAL DATABASE ON FAMILYSEARCH.ORG

1 Choose a database from the historical records list at **<www.familysearch.org/search/collection/location/1927074>**.

2 Fill in a name you want to search for (in this case, *Philip Heuschele*), then click Search at the bottom.

3 Review the search's results. Here, we have forty hits for *Philipp Heuschele*.

4 Click a result to see a card with the information in the record retrieved along with its source and citation (in this case, a FamilySearch microfilm of church records). Compare this information with what you already know about your ancestor to see if you've found a match.

Title ▾	Records	Last Updated	
Germany, Prussia, Westphalia, Minden, Miscellaneous Collections from the Municipal Archives, 1574-1902	22,580	15 Jan 2013	
Germany, Prussia, Pomerania Church Records, 1544-1945	185,216	22 Nov 2013	
Germany, Prussia, Brandenburg and Posen, Church Book Duplicates, 1794-1874	1,839,587	08 Oct 2015	
Germany, Mecklenburg-Schwerin Census, 1900	1,249,431	04 Jan 2011	
Germany, Mecklenburg-Schwerin Census, 1890	126,847	15 Apr 2014	
Germany, Mecklenburg-Schwerin Census, 1867	507,106	22 Aug 2014	
Germany, Hesse, Civil Registration, 1874-1927	77,265	24 Aug 2015	
Germany, Bremen Passenger Departure Lists, 1904-1914	44,315	17 Feb 2011	
Germany, Baden, Church Book Duplicates, 1800-1870	368,132	21 Aug 2015	
Germany Marriages, 1558-1929	8,521,369	18 Sep 2015	
Germany Deaths and Burials, 1582-1958	3,507,288	18 Sep 2015	
Germany Births and Baptisms, 1558-1898	37,703,403	18 Sep 2015	
Find A Grave Index	617,151	16 Nov 2014	
BillionGraves Index	181,705	07 Oct 2015	

2

RECORDS   GENEALOGIES   CATALOG   BOOKS   WIKI

Deutschland Geburten und Taufen, 1558-1898
Description

Index to selected Germany births and baptisms. Only a few localities are included and the time period varies by locality. Due to privacy laws, recent records may not be displayed. The year range represents most of the records. A few records may be earlier or later.

Learn more »

Search Collection

DECEASED ANCESTOR'S NAME

First Names — Philip
Last Names — Heuschele

Gender — Any

SEARCH WITH A LIFE EVENT:

Birth

Birthplace
Birth Year (Range) — From / To

SEARCH WITH A RELATIONSHIP:

Parents

RESTRICT RECORDS BY:

Type | Batch Number | Film Number

☐ Match all terms exactly

[Search]   Reset

3

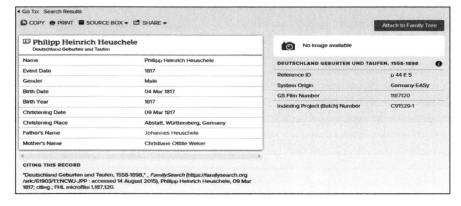

Deutschland Geburten und Taufen, 1558-1898

Refine your search

DECEASED ANCESTOR'S NAME

First Names — Philip
Last Names — Heuschele
Gender — Any

SEARCH WITH A LIFE EVENT:

Birthplace

Birth Year (Range) — From / To

1-20 of 40 results for >Name: **Philip Heuschele**

Number of results to show: 20 50 75

Name	Events		Relationships	
Philipp Heinrich Heuschele Germany Births and Baptisms, 1558-1898	birth: 4 March 1817 christening: 9 March 1817 — Abstatt, Württemberg, Germany residence: 1817 — Abstatt, Württemberg, Germany		father: Johannes Heuschele mother: Christiane Ottilie Weker	
Philipp Heinrich Heuschele Germany Births and Baptisms, 1558-1898	christening: 9 March 1817 — EVANGELISCH, ABSTATT, NECKARKREIS, WUERTTEMBERG		father: Johannes Heuschele mother: Christiane Ottilie Weker	
Philipp Heuschele Father Germany Births and Baptisms, 1558-1898			spouse: Anna Maria Schaeffer child: Helena Margareta Heuschele	

4

◀ Go To: Search Results

📋 COPY   🖨 PRINT   📦 SOURCE BOX ▾   ↗ SHARE ▾   [Attach to Family Tree]

Philipp Heinrich Heuschele
Deutschland Geburten und Taufen

Name	Philipp Heinrich Heuschele
Event Date	1817
Gender	Male
Birth Date	04 Mar 1817
Birth Year	1817
Christening Date	09 Mar 1817
Christening Place	Abstatt, Württemberg, Germany
Father's Name	Johannes Heuschele
Mother's Name	Christiane Ottilie Weker

📷 No image available

DEUTSCHLAND GEBURTEN UND TAUFEN, 1558-1898 ⓘ

Reference ID	p 44 E 5
System Origin	Germany-EASy
GS Film Number	1187120
Indexing Project (Batch) Number	C91529-1

CITING THIS RECORD

"Deutschland Geburten und Taufen, 1558-1898," , *FamilySearch* (https://familysearch.org /ark:/61903/1:1:NCWJ-JPP : accessed 14 August 2015), Philipp Heinrich Heuschele, 09 Mar 1817; citing ; FHL microfilm 1,187,120.

Image-Only Collections

Some four dozen sets of records consist of currently unindexed digitized collections. While about half of the collections in this category are either city directories or miscellaneous city records for many of Germany's midsize cities, a number of church and civil registers have been digitized, as well as a few military, probate, and Jewish records. As with the indexed collections, a number of databases will appeal to those looking for areas no longer within Germany.

Because urban immigrants are sometimes lost in the shuffle and therefore more difficult to document, the privately published city directories (*Adressbücher*) and other records in these collections can be helpful. While you'll notice considerable variance from city to city as far as what the collections marked "miscellaneous city records" contain, in a fair number of cases they include some of the following types of documents: marriage application documents, emigration records, citizen rolls, population registrations, local censuses, guardianship and adoption records, guild and apprenticeship records, and tax records.

The site has a number of digitized collections that include church and civil registers not previously microfilmed but still available through the FHL. Some of these contain only a few parishes' records. The largest quantity of such records in the digital collections are from the German states that now make up Hesse; however, most of these Hessian digitized records are not available for viewing on the Internet and require the user to look at them at a FamilySearch Center or to be a logged-in user of a partner organization (i.e., they must be a Church member). You can also find a number of indexes to funeral sermons, which serve as alternatives to death records.

In all cases, look carefully when you drill down into a digital collection and understand how large (or how limited) the offerings included are. One example is Germany, Hessen, Darmstadt, City Records, 1627–1940, which lists an invitingly broad date range for its collection of the documents from this midsize German city. Included in the collection are four types of records: *Aufnahmen von Bürgern und Beisassen* (records of citizenship and temporary residence), *Auswanderungen* (emigrants), *Bevölkerungsverhältnisse* (population list), and *Heimatscheine* (certificates of local citizenship). Only the population lists start in 1627; the others begin as late as the early 1800s.

Another database, Germany, Prussia, Pomerania, Stralsund, Church Book Indexes, 1600–1900, on the other hand, contains more than it advertises because it gives an abstract of the original records (that is, it includes more than just a name for the index entries, which are on scanned index cards) and also includes the town of Voigdehagen.

You'll recall that you can get a list of the image-only databases. While these collections may take longer to search, they still provide valuable information for your research. The following step-by-step takes you through to an individual database of records that has been digitized but not yet indexed.

STEP-BY-STEP EXAMPLE: SEARCHING AN IMAGE-ONLY COLLECTION ON FAMILYSEARCH.ORG

1 In the list of German image-only databases at **<www.familysearch.org/search/ collection/location/1927074>**, choose a particular collection of interest. Here we'll search for the first on the list: Germany, Anhalt, Dessau, City Directories, 1866–1919.

2 Click the link you'd like to see, and a general description of the database appears. On this screen, you can click Learn More for information about the source of the database or Browse Images to view what years or locations (or both) are available for each database.

3 Page through the database's images from your selected record type, year, and/or location. Use the arrows at the top of the page to move forward and back, or type a specific

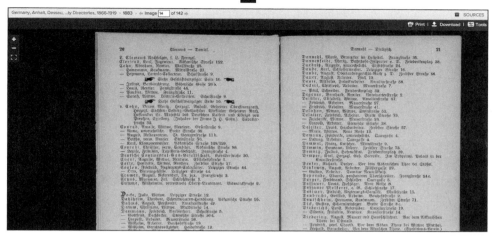

page number into the bar between the arrows. Once you've learned how the group of records you're browsing is organized, you may be able to skip ahead to pages where your ancestors may be located. For example, if you notice the records are arranged alphabetically and you're looking for an ancestor named *Schuster*, you can jump to a page halfway through the collection to save yourself having to click through all of the images.

OTHER ONLINE FEATURES

You may already be convinced that FamilySearch.org has a lot to offer German genealogy researchers, but there are many more ways the site can help you seek out *Deutsch* ancestors. Whether you seek additional background information, need to find offline materials held by the Church (and access them either at a local FamilySearch Center or in Salt Lake City), want to share information with others about your family trees, or mine the many family history surname books that have been published, FamilySearch.org can help you. We'll look at each of these aspects one by one.

FamilySearch Wiki and Learning Center

Literally hundreds of articles on the FamilySearch Wiki are relevant to German genealogy, profiling geographic areas, different record types, and even history. In many cases, the articles are written by FHL staff, many of whom have credentials in some way and all of whom are subject experts.

The Learning Center is accessed by clicking on Get Help in the upper right-hand corner of the FamilySearch.org home page, then selecting Learning Center under Self Help in the popup menu that results. The list for Germany on the left-hand side of the page shows about fifteen video courses. The courses, in a webinar format, include a variety of basic and intermediate topics. The center also includes other FamilySearch.org classes and links to classes and educational material elsewhere on the Web.

FamilySearch Catalog

We've given you a good taste of the types of German resources that FamilySearch.org has online, but the site is also the key to the full length and breadth of records that the FHL system has available in one medium or another. Many types of German record groups found online are also represented in the still-offline holdings: church and civil registers, tax lists,

Behind the Scenes: Volunteer Indexers

Volunteer indexing has been around for decades, and volunteers have been assisting with Mormon genealogy projects since 1921. Indexing started in many genealogical societies by going through a record or set of documents and noting the names or other items to be extracted on 3x5 index cards, then alphabetizing the cards.

But, just like so many things, it's come a long, long way!

In just the nine years of its existence, FamilySearch Indexing has taken volunteer transcription efforts to an unprecedented level via computer technology. In 2015 alone, more than a quarter-million contributed to the indexing effort, and more than one hundred million records were completed. Indeed, FamilySearch Indexing is well past the billion mark in total records completed.

The indexers, currently spread out working on about five hundred projects, are the ones whose work allows valuable genealogical records to be freely searchable online, making it perhaps the largest crowdsourcing effort of any type, anywhere. The projects vary in size and length, but FamilySearch Indexing attempts to post work every few months, even "publishing" (that is, posting the work on the FamilySearch.org site) partially indexed work on larger projects that take years.

Anyone—not just Church members—can join in the indexing effort, which can be accessed most easily by going directly to **<www.familysearch.org/indexing>**. Currently, participants download a program to use for indexing, and a browser-based indexing program is in the works. As a way of improving the indexing product, every image is indexed by two different indexers, and if they differ in their interpretation of the data, a third, specially trained indexer called an "arbitrator" breaks the tie on what the index should say about a record. Even with this auditing and a quality-control process, FamilySearch.org moves fast in making information available; FamilySearch Indexing currently publishes a project within ninety days of its completion.

It's truly a selfless effort that enables millions of FamilySearch.org users worldwide to easily find information they need in records.

land records such as hereditary leases (which can be especially valuable in areas such as Saxony where church record survival has been spotty), and so forth.

In addition, the catalog also details the microfilms, microfiche, books, and periodicals that often include histories of specific towns or regions, abstracts of historical records, and genealogies of towns and families. It also notes whether materials are in the digitized and/or indexed collections on FamilySearch.org.

While it's a superb compilation of the world's genealogical materials, the catalog has limitations that should be acknowledged. In any catalog of this size, there will be some inconsistencies in the subject headings under which the records are grouped. Some are easy to account for: When does a book on military history become one on military records, and how will it be categorized? A diligent researcher will obviously check for both. On the other hand, you could have the unlikely experience of finding Vital Records under Politics and Government, since those vital records are normally created by the government. (They can also be found under Church Records if they are the church book duplicates that were created by the churches but required by some German states as precursors to formal civil registrations.)

STEP-BY-STEP EXAMPLE: USING THE FAMILYSEARCH CATALOG

1 Go to the catalog's home page at <www.familysearch.org/catalog-search> or by hovering over Search on the site's main toolbar and clicking Catalog. There, you'll see that you can search by Place, Surnames, Titles, Author, Subjects, or Keywords. You can also search for a specific call number for a book or film/fiche number for those media. For example, you might see a citation for an FHL microfilm number and want to know a specific rundown of what is contained on that film.

2 Choose the type of search you want to perform. Place is the default, and that's what we'll use. As you fill in the name of the place, the catalog will attempt to match it with known places programmed in the catalog. Two things of note: First, the catalog entry will come back in most instances showing generally Second German Empire (1871–1918) boundaries of "nation, state, county (or equivalent), town," but you only need to include a town name. Secondly, the catalog ignores umlauts (that is, you don't have to account for the umlaut in typing) but will show the town name as umlauted, if it is.

3 If the catalog has matched more than one possible place to what you've typed (in this example, *Sprendlingen*), choose one of the possibilities.

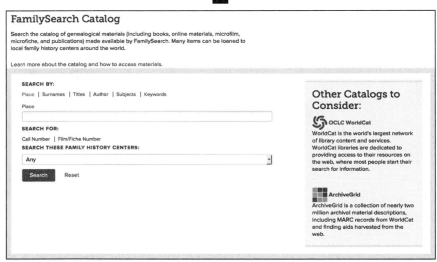

1

FamilySearch Catalog

Search the catalog of genealogical materials (including books, online materials, microfilm, microfiche, and publications) made available by FamilySearch. Many items can be loaned to local family history centers around the world.

Learn more about the catalog and how to access materials.

SEARCH BY:

Place | Surnames | Titles | Author | Subjects | Keywords

Place

SEARCH FOR:

Call Number | Film/Fiche Number

SEARCH THESE FAMILY HISTORY CENTERS:

Any

Search   Reset

Other Catalogs to Consider:

OCLC WorldCat

WorldCat is the world's largest network of library content and services. WorldCat libraries are dedicated to providing access to their resources on the web, where most people start their search for information.

ArchiveGrid

ArchiveGrid is a collection of nearly two million archival material descriptions, including MARC records from WorldCat and finding aids harvested from the web.

2

SEARCH BY:

Place | Surnames | Titles | Author | Subjects | Keywords

Place

SEARCH FOR:

Call Number | Film/Fiche Number

SEARCH THESE FAMILY HISTORY CENTERS:

Any

Search   Reset

3

SEARCH BY:

Place | Surnames | Titles | Author | Subjects | Keywords

Place

Sprendling

Sprendlingen (Kr. Alzey)

Germany, Hessen, Sprendlingen (Kr. Alzey)

Sprendlingen (Kr. Offenbach)

Germany, Hessen, Sprendlingen (Kr. Offenbach)

2 Results

4 A

Search Results for FamilySearch Catalog

🖨 PRINT 📋 Catalog Print List (0)

Part of Germany, Hessen

▸ Germany, Hessen, Sprendlingen (Kr. Alzey) - Church records (4)   Print List

4 B

Search Results for FamilySearch Catalog

🖨 PRINT 📋 Catalog Print List (0)

Part of Germany, Hessen

▾ **Germany, Hessen, Sprendlingen (Kr. Alzey) - Church records** (4)   Print List

Kirchenbuch, 1581-1897	Add
Author: Evangelische Kirche Sprendlingen (Kr. Alzey)	
Kirchenbuch, 1672-1798	Add
Author: Evangelische Kirche Sprendlingen (Kr. Alzey)	
Kirchenbuch, 1692-1934	Add
Author: Katholische Kirche Sprendlingen (Kr. Alzey)	
Kirchenbuchduplikat, 1819-1875	Add
Author: Evangelische Kirche Sprendlingen (Kr. Alzey)	

4 After you choose from the possibilities presented, hit Search. The search results will be displayed in categories—in this case, four sets of church records for *Sprendlingen* (image **4 A**). Click on the arrow to the left of the search results to identify individual results and bring up the details on that title, which sometimes will be found on multiple microfilms (image **4 B**).

ORDERING MICROFILMS TO A FAMILYSEARCH CENTER

The Church operates a network of FamilySearch Centers around the country (often in local Church branches or buildings) that can be your "close-to-home away from home" for microfilmed resources that haven't yet been digitized. To use it, you'll need to register for a free FamilySearch account. Once you do that, choose a FamilySearch Center where you want to view your films; FamilySearch calls this your default center. Since different centers have varying hours and technology capabilities (scanning, printing, etc.), you probably want to check out those things (if more than one center is within a reasonable distance) before choosing your default center. You can find more information on the FamilySearch Centers on the bottom left-hand side of the FamilySearch.org home page.

PLANNING FHL RESEARCH

Despite the oodles of online resources we've been telling you about, you still have substantial reasons to make the trek to Utah. Reason number one is to tap into the expertise of the FHL staff, as sometimes a personal explanation of records, organization schema, or results beats computer correspondence. And, of course, you may want to use the online FamilySearch Catalog to plan offline research at the FHL in Salt Lake City. You can put together lists of microfilms and books you want to examine well in advance of your trip. Another good strategy would be to connect with library staff ahead of the visit to make sure the specialist you need will be available during the time you're in Salt Lake City. When you search the online catalog, you'll also want to take note of any microfilms marked as being in the vault, since these microfilms need to be retrieved from off-site storage and therefore should be ordered immediately upon arrival.

FAMILY TREES AND COMMUNITY TREES

You can keep track of your research and create a profile of your ancestor by making a family tree on FamilySearch.org. Go to the Family Tree tab on the FamilySearch.org home page, then compare your existing family tree to others in the FamilySearch Family Tree database. Unlike most other websites, FamilySearch.org is working towards "one tree," in which all family trees are interconnected and each person in the site's family trees has a unique ID number. As a result, your family tree is, in a way, for the whole FamilySearch.org community; anyone can view or change information about deceased individuals on your tree or connect their cultivated family tree to yours. In addition, FamilySearch.org's Family Tree function has many tools to add sources, comments, photos, stories, video, and audio clips to your ancestor's profile. The Family Tree also uses a software called Puzzilla **<www.puzzilla.org>** that gives nifty assistance with descendancy research (that is, probing into cousins of your ancestors).

Fed up with searching for records yourself? Try turning to family trees published by others. Under the Search tab, select Genealogies and search the databases there, including Ancestral File, the Pedigree Resource File, the International Genealogical Index (which we'll discuss later in this chapter), and Community Trees. You can search all of these at once, but be aware that Ancestral File and Pedigree Resource File, which are mostly user submitted, are filled with many

POWER-USER TIP

Carefully Plant Your Family Tree
FamilySearch's Family Tree has the laudable goal of having only one profile per person. However, with the many different skill levels among genealogists using the service, deciding whose data trumps whose can be a nightmare. Take caution when viewing other people's trees. You never know how much (or rather, how little) research they've done to support their ancestor's profile.

duplicate trees and unsourced entries. They can be valuable for clues to real records but are inherently unreliable. Community Trees pull from well-sourced trees compiled by FamilySearch.org staff in attempts to create full-town genealogies.

You can also look at other users' pedigrees. Go to the Family Tree menu on the FamilySearch.org home page and click Find to search other users' trees for your ancestor. Note that if you have already started a computer pedigree in other software and want to upload it to FamilySearch.org while avoiding double-keyboarding, you need to upload it here at the Genealogies tab under the Search menu rather than under Family Tree.

INTERNATIONAL GENEALOGICAL INDEX

The venerable International Genealogical Index (IGI) merits a separate section from the Ancestral File and Pedigree Resource File databases because many of the entries in the IGI database were extractions from baptismal and marriage records found in German church registers. Therefore, it's a much more reliable database than the other two (which were based on submissions from users who often supplied no sources for the information included) and still has ways of helping you with your research.

Sometimes using the IGI is a way of "turning down the noise" of everything found in a full-fledged FamilySearch.org sweep. And even if your particular ancestor isn't found in the IGI, running a search of the surname you're looking for (as long as it's not too common) may yield some helpful hotspots—villages or areas of Germany in which the surname is found. Go to **<www.familysearch.org/search/collection/igi>** to search just the IGI.

Family History Books

The first thing to know about this collection is that, unlike its name might imply, Family History Books contains more than just books. It's a collection of nearly two hundred thousand digitized genealogy and family history publications (including magazines, monographs, and of course books) thanks to a collaborative effort between FamilySearch's FHL, the Allen County (Indiana) Public Library, the Houston Public Library's Clayton Library Center, the Mid-Continent (Missouri) Public Library's Midwest Genealogy

Center, the Historical Society of Pennsylvania, Brigham Young University campus libraries, and several other repositories.

The collection (image **E**) includes family histories, county and local histories, genealogy magazines and how-to books, gazetteers, and medieval histories and pedigrees. Some of the items can be accessed from home computers, but others are covered by restrictions that require the user to be in the FHL, a FamilySearch Center, or one of the partner libraries to access to the digital copies. For books still under copyright, only one user worldwide can access such a book at any one time (since that's legally the same as using the book at the original library).

Searching the database can be done from anywhere, and the every-word search capability at least allows users to get more detailed information on what printed sources may contain and if it's of interest. Using the Advanced Search form (image **F**) allows users a number of options to narrow down hits to a reasonable number by limiting searches to such items as titles or publications that contain certain words or phrases.

TIPS, CAVEATS, AND FORECASTS

The future of FamilySearch.org seems easy to predict: more, more, and more! Well, more of everything except microfilm, but that will in turn feed the "more" for the online side of the Mormons' genealogy effort. The change from microfilm to full digital storage—predicted to take as long as a century when it was first initiated less than a decade ago!—now has an estimated completion date of the end of the decade.

One reason for that acceleration has been the partnerships FamilySearch has built with the for-profit end of the genealogy block, namely Ancestry.com **<www.ancestry.com>** and MyHeritage **<www.myheritage.com>**, which have invested heavily in helping FamilySearch.org digitize the remaining microfilms. In exchange, those for-pay services acquired the right to also show many of the FamilySearch.org collections on their own subscription sites.

Unless FamilySearch is able to negotiate new contracts with the owners of "restricted" microfilms (mostly, for our purposes, German church and civil archives), those digital products will remain usable only at the FHL in Salt Lake City or by visiting FamilySearch Centers. While it would be great to see such renegotiation, don't bet on it: Many German archives look at their records as revenue sources (as you'll see in chapter 8 about Archion **<www.archion.de>**, the new Protestant church records for-pay site) rather than believe that this kind of public information should be broadly available. The likely result is that a substantial number of the digital films will require researchers to go to FamilySearch Centers, which hopefully will see an uptick in resources to help researchers after a num-

E

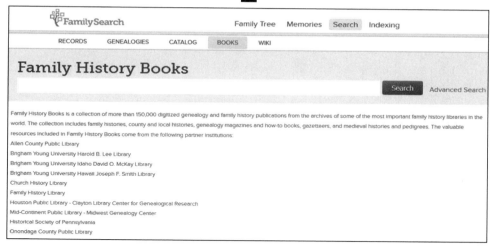

F

ber of years of neglect (presumably because so many people want to do genealogy strictly at home).

With the current microfilm rental system, a patron orders films, waits for them to be mailed to the FamilySearch Center, views them, then needs to start the whole process over again if, say, the records show that the ancestor's parents came from a different village. With digital viewing, the researcher will be able to move on to a new digitized film as if he or she were in Salt Lake City!

While this process continues, FamilySearch is also putting into place features such as "thumbnail galleries" (which allow users to browse indexed entries and the digital original records together) as well as icons in the online catalog to indicate what medium or media (microfilm or digital images) a particular item currently can be accessed on. FamilySearch is also accelerating its effort to reduce the time lag (currently around ninety days) between indexing and publishing those indexes on the site; the indexing arm hopes to dramatically cut that lag over the next couple of years. Not only that, but the browser-based indexing program that's in the works will allow indexers to "work in the cloud" instead of downloading a separate program. The exciting debut of a "community indexing tool" that allows users to add comments and make clarifications or corrections to indexed data collections is also on FamilySearch.org's horizon.

The partnerships that FamilySearch has forged are likely to continue since the money that the for-profit outfits can add to the mix is important in getting rights to records and paying for the digitization process. In addition, as the mover behind the RootsTech conference now held annually in Salt Lake City, FamilySearch is encouraging technological innovation on all genealogy fronts. Some technologies in very early stages of development even attempt to use OCR (optical character recognition, which is how most indexing of books and newspapers is now accomplished) to create indexing for German script documents. With FamilySearch's track record, it wouldn't be surprising for the organization to help lead such an effort, which would create the next revolution of access to millions of handwritten records.

KEYS TO SUCCESS

▓ Know what German research resources are available to you for free on FamilySearch.org, and how and where to access them. Most of FamilySearch.org's online record collections include either a searchable index or images of the records, but often not both.

▓ Remember that FamilySearch.org has much more to offer than its stockpile of digitized records. Search Family Tree Books for digitized publications and the Genealogies section for other users' family trees, the Ancestral File, the Pedigree Resource File, and the IGI.

▓ Use the Learning Center and FamilySearch Wiki, curated by experts in the field, to learn more about Germanic history and language, your research, and what records are available to you.

▓ Identify and request resources in different kinds of media using the FamilySearch Catalog. If you find a title that's only in print, see if the publication can be loaned to your local FamilySearch Center.

FAMILYSEARCH RECORDS CHECKLIST

Ancestor's name: _____

Ancestor's maiden name (if female): _____

Date of birth: _____ Birthplace: _____

Residence/location: _____

Spouse's name: _____

Children's names: _____

European Records Search Checklist

☐ Look at the Historical Records Collections list **<www.familysearch.org/search/collection/list>**. Filter by Place and select Germany.

☐ Identify collections to search or browse that cover your ancestor's location and time period. (You may need to click on the collection title, then the Learn More link, to determine if the location covers your ancestor's province or town.)

☐ Search indexed collections.

☐ Browse unindexed collections.

FamilySearch.org Indexed Records Search Tracker

Collection Title and Date Coverage	Date Searched	Search Criteria Used	Results/Notes

FamilySearch.org Unindexed Records Search Tracker

If the browsable record image collection you're looking at has index pages (but hasn't been fully indexed), use these divisions to your advantage, then use this form to track your browsing efforts. Fill in these boxes with each index you find to help keep track of possible record images that list your ancestors. You can download a Word-document version of this worksheet at <ftu.familytreemagazine.com/trace-your-german-roots-online>.

Surnames to research: _____

Collection title: _____

Record type: _____

Location: _____

Year: _____

Surnames Found on Index	Record Number	Digital Record Image Page Number

5

ANCESTRY.COM: THE ULTIMATE *ÜBER*-SITE

Nearly all of my ancestors resided in the Pennsylvania German heartland of Berks County in 1850. So one of my first genealogical acts after becoming engrossed in the hobby in the mid-1980s was seeking out the microfilms of the 1850 US census and seizing what turned out to be three films for Berks at the nearest repository where I was living at the time.

I recall spending eight hours and getting "microfilm reader elbow" from scrolling through just that trio of films and copying down the couple dozen direct-line ancestral families I had found—though I admit that it took longer because I didn't know how to use the coding that a local society had produced! It was a wonderfully exciting but exhausting day—but who would access the census that way in the present? Just as a test, I found and printed out those same family records in just fifty-three minutes using the Ancestry.com search engine **<search.ancestry.com>** as an index.

A subscription to Ancestry.com **<www.ancestry.com>** is an essential component of any German genealogist's research regimen. Yes, the site has limitations and some shortfalls to bear in mind, and we'll point these out in this chapter. But on balance, it's not a close call to say that, with the price of its highest-end subscription still about a buck a day when paid annually, Ancestry.com is one of the genealogy world's true bargains. Without the investment made by its original founding partners and subscribers to Ancestry.com over the years, considerably fewer (if any) records would be available to genealogists on the Internet. And when you factor in the time and transportation savings when comparing using the site to going to repositories or trying to use only free sites, it's hard to argue that Ancestry doesn't pay for itself—and then some.

In this chapter, we'll review some basics about Ancestry.com, school you in what comes free of charge on the site (including a valuable pre-WWI German gazetteer), go through Ancestry.com's voluminous grab bag of German genealogy content, and also mention some of the goodies on Ancestry.com sister sites such as Newspapers.com **<www.newspapers.com>**, Fold3 **<www.fold3.com>**, and the venerable RootsWeb **<www.rootsweb.ancestry.com>**. For more detail about Ancestry.com and how to use it, see the *Unofficial Guide to Ancestry.com* by Nancy Hendrickson (Family Tree Books, 2014) **<www.shopfamilytree.com/unofficial-guide-to-ancestry>**.

SITE OVERVIEW

As far as size and complexity, Ancestry.com is another monolith of a website like FamilySearch.org **<www.familysearch.org>**, which we discussed in chapter 4. A lot of the similarity ends at that point, however, since Ancestry.com is a for-profit company (though it's gone through various business structures in its existence). And while it has made considerable attempts at helping the largely nonprofit genealogy community, it *is* a business, and some of its moves over the years have been decidedly less than friendly to some segments of the genealogy world.

Ancestry.com offers three different membership levels, and the *Unofficial Guide* goes into detail about them. For this book's purposes, you need to know the following: You can access the free items and create a family tree on Ancestry.com by registering (for free) as an Ancestry Member, but you'll need to have the World Explorer or All Access membership to access some of the German records referred to here. You can learn about the three tiers of paid subscription service online **<www.ancestry.com/cs/offers/subscribe?sub=1>**. Ancestry.com occasionally runs fourteen-day free trials of its memberships, a great way to get acquainted with the site and its value before investing more time and money. You can also receive a discounted plan if you pay semiannually rather than monthly, and AARP members receive a one-time discount.

In addition to being able to select from different tiers of membership plans, you can choose which elements will appear on your Ancestry.com home page to suit your research needs. Across the top of your screen, you'll see a menu with six broad categories. **Home** takes you to your Ancestry.com home page, which you can customize, and you can create, manage, or upload your own family tree in **Trees**. You'll likely spend most of your time on the site in Search, which gives you a submenu of general record categories that will be detailed later. For those interested in genetic genealogy or who have taken a DNA test, **DNA** takes you into the burgeoning AncestryDNA arm of the company **<dna.ancestry.com>**. The **Help** submenu contains links to the Support Center (for technical questions) and the Learning Center, which includes downloadable research guides. Under Help, you can also access Community and Message Boards to collaborate with other Ancestry.com users and the World Archives Project, an ongoing project dedicated to indexing all records. Finally, **Extras** includes links to download Ancestry.com apps for iOS and Android, create and order photo projects, browse Ancestry Academy (a collection of video courses), and buy gift subscriptions. You can connect with ProGenealogists

A

Ancestry.com's general search form will comb through the site's millions of records, though the number of results may overwhelm you.

(professional researchers who work for hire) under both tabs: Hire an Expert under Help and ProGenealogists under Extras.

As stated earlier, most of the heavy lumber for German genealogists will be found under the Search tab. If you just click on Search, you'll arrive at a generic search form (image **A**) for you to fill out, though an advanced search form is available, too. While you'll eventually dig deeper into individual records collections, you'll want to run your ancestors through this as a starting point. If you just click on the Search tab, you'll find a list of record collections (categories of similar records consisting of many individual Ancestry.com databases) and other searchable data that includes:

- **All Collections:** As the title implies, this directory searches all of Ancestry.com's databases in one fell swoop. The downside here, especially for German researchers looking for surnames with many spelling variants, is that the results you might actually want get lost in the clutter of this all-inclusive search.

- **Census & Voter Lists:** Here's where you get the entire run of the publicly available US census listings (as well as UK censuses, too). The available US censuses that list names for everyone in the household (1850 to 1940, though most of 1890 has been lost) are probably the most important building blocks for American genealogy research. Their listings for birthplace (and other information such as country of origin and native tongue, depending upon the year) are helpful to German genealogists.

- **Birth, Marriage & Death:** These records mark your ancestors' most pivotal events (hence, "vital" records). Marriage records and especially death records may list information helpful to proving when and where your ancestors came over from Europe.

- **Immigration & Travel:** Included here are the National Archives and Records Administration passenger arrival lists (from 1820 for most ports) as well as databases on Colonial arrivals. The collection also includes naturalization records from many jurisdictions; these records, of course, indicate immigration and sometimes will provide European hometowns.

- **Public Member Trees:** Ancestry.com subscribers and members have flocked to provide family tree information, though their findings can be based on anything from good primary research to cut-and-paste jobs from someone else's unsourced trees. If nothing else, their trees can be good starting points.

- **Military:** Here you can access databases of draft cards from both world wars as well as records from the Civil War. More military records are found on Fold3, an Ancestry.com property that specializes in them.

- **Card Catalog:** This is Ancestry.com's "drill down" tool you can use to search or browse individual databases instead of the whole megadose of names. More on how this works after these bullet points are finished!

- **Member Directory:** Using this function might take you back to days of yore (you know, about twenty years ago), when a fair number of genealogy societies published surname indexes of families their members were searching for. In the Ancestry.com directory, you can search by last name, first name, or username by using the Find a specific member field. Or you can search by surname, location, and year of study by searching the Find members researching... field. Both searches return a list of members' usernames, research interests, "member since" date, and a time frame of when they last signed in (the latter to presumably judge whether someone may be a member but no longer active in genealogy).

The Card Catalog

Back to the Card Catalog for a moment. The Card Catalog is a key part of Ancestry.com for two reasons. While it's not quite like the local library card catalogs of an earlier day—it's not the old trio of subject, title, and author headings—it's a way to seek out specific databases or databases with particular information. Secondly, it's your entrée into browsing digitized images of the specific databases.

Instead of subject, title, and author headings, the Ancestry.com Card Catalog has two prime search boxes. First, there's Title, which as you might expect will return databases with a particular word in the title (you can use an asterisk to substitute for letters—for instance, *German** will come back with results for databases with either *Germany* or *German* in the title). Secondly, there's Keyword(s), which can be part of the title but are also drawn from metadata describing the database and therefore are broader (asterisks can be used here, too, to widen the search). Once you've done a search, you'll also see other filters available—by collection, by location, by dates, or by languages—if you want to narrow the number of databases further.

There's no one magic title or keyword, however, that gets you all the German genealogy resources at once; for example, the *German** title and keyword searches do successfully pick up a number of the Ancestry.com databases for church records of ethnic German congregations in America, but not all of them. You'll also want to do searches for names of specific villages and German states if you are searching individual databases (though again, you should first do a global search of all the site's databases from the main Search tab—searching more narrowly in databases will help you whittle down that unwieldy number of results). Unlike FamilySearch.org's consistent use of the states of Second German Empire to label villages (see chapter 4), Ancestry.com's catalog some-times uses state names and other times does not.

For pretty much anything you find on Ancestry.com, you'll have the opportunity to send it to a shoebox as part of your customized Ancestry site or download the record (or book page, or whatever) to your own computer. You'll also find that when you do global searches on Ancestry.com or start a family tree on the site, the site will try to help you out by offering shaking leaf icons (hints) that show records that may relate to the same individual. The shaking leaves should be used with caution; sometimes they can be a great research shortcut, but other times they will only relate to your ancestor because they have a similar name.

STEP-BY-STEP EXAMPLE: SEARCHING FOR DATABASES IN THE ANCESTRY.COM CARD CATALOG

1 From the top menu at Ancestry.com, click Search. Click on Card Catalog from the drop-down menu.

2 On the Card Catalog page, use the Title and Keyword(s) boxes to drill down your search. For example, fill in *German* in the Title field and click Search.

3 View your results and click a database to search or browse. In this example, search-ing *German* resulted in sixty-nine databases (such as German Phone Directories, 1915–1981, and German Casualties in the Franco-Prussian War, 1870–1871) instead of the thirty-three thousand you would have received from a general search of the site.

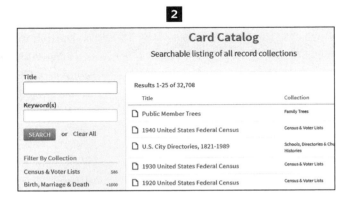

WHAT COMES FREE OF CHARGE

Though there's no doubt that Ancestry.com's worth any serious German genealogist's subscription dollars, some substantial resources are available merely by registering for free as an Ancestry Member. These freebies include the pre-WWI *Meyers Gazetteer of the German Empire* <search.ancestry.com/search/db.aspx?dbid=1074> that is so useful for finding data on German villages, plus several worthwhile emigration databases as well as indexes to some records and even a database of historical postcards. Several of these items deserve a more detailed look.

Meyers Gazetteer

Ancestry's Card Catalog calls it the *Meyers Gazetteer of the German Empire*, but naturally the Germans have a longer name for it: *Meyers Orts- und Verkehrs-Lexikon des Deutschen Reichs*. No matter what name you give it, this research tool is indispensable to German genealogists because it was published in the early 1900s, during the Second German Empire period (1871–1918) when Germany encompassed its great peacetime territory.

In addition to containing hundreds of thousands of entries as a geographical dictionary, *Meyers* includes loads of information about the places included: the state and district

POWER-USER TIP

Carefully Read Labels
Be wary of the geographic designations on the scanned pages in databases (both German and American). Some reflect mistaken and misspelled names in the originals; other errors may have been introduced when metadata was added.

to which it belongs; whether it had its own civil registration office (or where its vital records were registered if not); population; court and military district data; businesses and industries; and whether there were churches in the town (and of what denomination). This is a case where the language skills that previous chapters have encouraged become helpful; of course, *Meyers* is in German and also printed in the difficult-to-read Fraktur font. You'll also likely want to invest in a copy of the late Wendy K. Uncapher's still-in-print monograph *How to Read & Understand Meyers Orts- und Verkehrs-Lexikon des Deutschen Reichs* (Origins, 2003) to help understand the heavily abbreviated listings of the villages.

STEP-BY-STEP EXAMPLE: USING THE *MEYERS GAZETTEER*

1 Enter *Meyers Gazetteer* on the Card Catalog search page. The *Meyers* database comes up as the only database that meets the criteria. Click it to access the record.

2 On the resulting page, you can Search (entering a town name for which you are looking) or Browse (going directly to the scanned images, divided in alphabetical order). For the purpose of this demonstration, the Search function is difficult to use, so we'll demonstrate Browse.

3 To browse the collection, enter the first letter of the name of the place you're seeking (for example, *C*). The beginning and ending place names for the pages of the gazetteer will then be displayed (the first few pages of the letter *C* are displayed). Click on the page you wish to view.

4 Browse the database's images. Navigate from one page to the other by using either the arrows in the toolbar or by typing in a page number into the field and hitting Enter to jump to that page.

1

Card Catalog
Searchable listing of all record collections

Title				
Meyers Gazetteer	Results 1-1 of 1		Sort By	Popularity
	Title	Collection	Records	Activity
Keyword(s)				
	🗋 Meyers Gazetteer of the German Empire (in German)	Maps, Atlases & Gazetteers	201,829	
SEARCH or Clear All				1

2

3

4

Free Indexes

A good number of the Ancestry.com freebies for German genealogists are merely indexes of collections, which makes sense from a business standpoint; if you want to access the original records, you'll have to ante up. But the impressive thing is that these are a first-class tease, since the indexes the site includes are for some substantial emigration indexes from a couple of German states as well as some marriages and the seldom-seen helpful German state censuses. Among the databases that have free indexes are the following:

- Baden, Germany Emigration Index, 1866–1911 **<search.ancestry.com/search/ db.aspx?dbid=4610>**: An index of emigrants from this southwestern German state over a forty-five-year period

- Lübeck, Germany, Census Indexes: Separate databases for nearly a dozen head counts taken in this northern German city-state between 1807 and 1862

- Lübeck, Germany, Marriage Banns, 1871–1875 **<search.ancestry.com/search/ db.aspx?dbid=1567>**: Marriage records predating the advent of civil registers in Germany

- Mecklenburg-Schwerin, Germany, Census, 1919 **<search.ancestry.com/search/ db.aspx?dbid=1794>**: A census from this northern German state

- Wuerttemberg, Germany Emigration Index **<search.ancestry.com/search/ db.aspx?dbid=3141>**: Some sixty thousand names of those leaving from the former kingdom situated between Baden and Bavaria in southern Germany, compiled by the legendary German researcher Trudy Schenk

Roundup of Other Free Items

In some cases, the actual records in the Ancestry databases are free for the taking. Significant such databases include:

- Brandenburg, Prussia Emigration Records **<search.ancestry.com/search/ db.aspx?dbid=4121>**: Includes more than sixty thousand names of emigrants as compiled by expert researcher Marion Wolfert

- Germany & Austria Historical Postcards **<search.ancestry.com/search/ db.aspx?dbid=1120>**: More than twenty-five thousand historical postcards with photos of places in Germany and Austria, searchable by location or keyword—you may well find a postcard or two mentioning the *Heimat* you're researching!

In addition, Ancestry.com has made a number of databases dealing with the German death camps and deportations of Jews from Germany during the WWII era free.

Timeline of the Hamburg Embarkation Lists

The Hamburg Embarkation Lists and their Handwritten Indexes are two separate databases that Ancestry has obtained from the state archives of Hamburg. Here's a chronology of the lists and handwritten indexes and what's available for searching and browsing:

1850	Embarkation lists begin, initially just with names of passengers (first names often just had an initial) but later with additional details. Ancestry.com has also made available images for the entire extant run of lists.
1855	Handwritten indexes begin. Because the database is an index, these are not searchable on Ancestry.com and are only browsable.
1854–1910	The lists and handwritten indexes are separated into "direct" (passengers who weren't going to change ships before their ultimate arrivals) and "indirect" (those who did change ships).
1911	Lists are no longer separated into "direct" and "indirect."
1915–1919	No lists are kept during World War I.
1934	Lists and indexes from the port of Hamburg are no longer produced.

MAJOR UNIQUE ASSETS

Naturally enough, which of Ancestry.com's assets are considered "major" for German genealogy is in the eye of the beholder; value, to some extent, is going to depend on whether your ancestors are found in a particular record set. Still and all, plenty of databases are unique to Ancestry.com, covering a multitude of times and places. Only the rare German researcher would be unable to find databases to mine, especially when you take into consideration databases including church records of ethnic Germans in America.

Another criterion is whether an asset can be found somewhere else on the Internet (especially if it's for free on FamilySearch.org). The best examples are the huge databases of German births, marriages, and deaths. These include millions of records—but they are the same databases compiled by FamilySearch. (Interestingly enough, when Ancestry.com counts the "records" for each of these megadatabases, it comes up with three times as many as FamilySearch.org, presumably because the site segments the pieces of data included in the database's documents in a different way.) Likewise, Ancestry.com has a couple dozen databases that FamilySearch.org designates as "miscellaneous city records" that are also duplicated on Ancestry.com because of the two groups' partnership.

But while the caveat to look for content first on FamilySearch.org is valid enough, Ancestry.com has a bunch of intriguing databases that you won't find there (or anywhere else, for that matter). This is where the rubber hits the road for Ancestry.com and the German genealogist—or perhaps a better metaphor is where the "ship hits the water," since the number one marquee item is the Hamburg Embarkation Lists and their manuscript indexes.

Hamburg Embarkation Lists

The star attractions of Ancestry.com's major assets are the records of emigration departures from the German port of Hamburg, which was the number two exit point from the European continent in the 1800s. About five million people left from Hamburg between 1850 and 1934 (the years that records were kept for), and about a third of those who left from Hamburg were from the German states. The remainder were from other areas, primarily eastern Europe, including many from the Russian Empire as well as Austria-Hungary.

You'll want to check out two specific databases if you have ancestors who left Europe in the second half of the 1800s or early in the 1900s: Hamburg Passenger Lists, 1850–1934 **<search.ancestry.com/search/db.aspx?dbid=1068>** and Hamburg Passenger Lists, Handwritten Indexes, 1855–1934 **<search.ancestry.com/search/db.aspx?dbid=1166>**.

While the database with images of the actual lists is searchable for the years 1850 to 1923 (the entire run of images is available), bad handwriting creates a hide-and-seek game in which you may not be able to find who you're looking for even with creative searches. In that case, you'll want to browse the database of handwritten indexes in an attempt to find the name you're looking for, then find it in the actual lists. You'll either need to have a focused time period—or a lot of time on your hands!—since the handwritten indexes are segmented chronologically and then further broken up just by first letter of the last name. A further wrinkle is that for a portion of their run, the lists were divided into "direct" (passengers staying on the same ship to their ultimate arrival port) and "indirect" (those switching ships, usually somewhere in the British Isles).

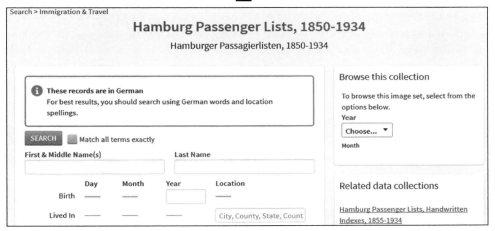

STEP-BY-STEP EXAMPLE: USING THE HAMBURG EMBARKATION LISTS AND INDEXES

1 From the Card Catalog screen, fill in the Title field with *Hamburg Passenger*. The search will return both (and only) the Hamburg lists and handwritten indexes. Click on which database you'd like to search: Go to step 2 for the Hamburg lists database or step 3 for the handwritten indexes database.

2 The Hamburg Passengers List database gives you the option to Search (on the left) or Browse (on the right). As with other search forms, you can use special characters to account for some spelling variations, but you'll likely have mixed results when keyword searching because of bad handwriting. If you can't find something useful in either way and you know an approximate time period of embarkation, try the handwritten indexes database.

Hamburg Passenger Lists, Handwritten Indexes, 1855-1934

Hamburger Passagierlisten, handschriftliche Indizes, 1855-1934

Source Information

Ancestry.com. *Hamburg Passenger Lists, Handwritten Indexes, 1855-1934* [database on-line]. Provo, UT, USA: Ancestry.com Operations Inc, 2007.

Original data: Staatsarchiv Hamburg, Bestand: 373-7 I, VIII (Auswanderungsamt I). Mikrofilmrollen K 1871 - K 1962, S 17363 - S 17383, 13174 - 13183.

Browse this collection

To browse this image set, select from the options below.

Year

Choose... ▼

Band
▼

Surname Letter

---

3 The Hamburg Passenger Lists, Handwritten Indexes database is not electronically searchable; you need to "browse" it by time period on the right-hand side. First, choose Year (a set of years), then Band (volume) opens up and narrows to time frame. Finally, choose the Surname Letter (the first letter of the surname). If you find someone, you need to go back to the actual passenger lists and browse them based on the information you gained from the handwritten indexes (personal name, ship name, date, etc.).

Records from the Historical Society of Pennsylvania

Ancestry.com has digitized an enormous database of millions of records (almost eleven million using Ancestry.com's math) that includes many church records relevant to those researching "first wave" (Colonial era) Germans in the Mid-Atlantic states, called Pennsylvania and New Jersey, Church and Town Records, 1708–1985 **<search.ancestry.com/search/db.aspx?dbid=2451>**. Most of the eighteenth-century records in this collection focus on baptisms, marriages, and burials, though a few other types of records such as confirmations are available for some congregations.

These records primarily come from microfilms in the custody of the Historical Society of Pennsylvania (HSP) **<www.hsp.org>**. And many of these were acquired due to the HSP's relationship with the Genealogical Society of Pennsylvania **<genpa.org>**. In addition to original church registers, this database also includes many transcriptions of cemetery tombstone inscriptions and is both searchable and browsable on Ancestry.com. The browse function allows you to drill down first by county, then "city" (which sometimes needs to be massaged because many of these are country churches), and finally denomination (religious group) and name of the specific church.

Records from Evangelical Lutheran Archives

What the HSP collection is for the "first wavers," the records of the Evangelical Lutheran Church in America are to the "second wave" Germans, many of whom settled in the American Midwest. The database is called U.S., Evangelical Lutheran Church of America, Records, 1875–1940 <search.ancestry.com/search/db.aspx?dbid=60722>, and contains more membership lists, records of communion, and treasures' reports in addition to the "big three" (baptism, marriage, burial) records. Like the HSP collection, this database is both searchable and browsable. When browsing, you can view records by state, then city and specific congregation (in larger cities where there was more than one Lutheran church).

Brandenburg Church Records Transcripts

The powerhouse database titled Brandenburg, Germany, Transcripts of Church Records, 1700–1874 <search.ancestry.com/search/db.aspx?dbid=2116>, contains records from hundreds of parishes in the old Prussian heartland of Brandenburg, which overlaps but does not exactly correspond with the current German *Land* by that name—indeed, historic Brandenburg includes some areas now in Poland, a difficult-to-research area. Most of the records are from *Evangelisch* congregations, although some Roman Catholic and "Old Lutheran" records are also included. The source information attached to the database also gives a complete list of the parishes—as well as the names of all the villages included in those parishes—as part of the source information. The database is both searchable and browsable.

Ansbach Lutheran Parish Register Extracts

The database Ansbach, Germany, Lutheran Parish Register Extracts, 1550–1920 <search.ancestry.com/search/db.aspx?dbid=60913>, is similar to the Brandenburg collection in that it does not contain original church records, but, in many cases, is easier to read than the original set of records. The extracts on Ancestry.com are searchable and browsable. The Ansbach district's original records are part of the Protestant church record supersite Archion **<archion.de>**, which will be profiled in chapter 8.

Various Civil Registers

Ancestry.com has a geographically scattered but growing number of databases with digitized civil registers of births, marriages, and deaths, usually up to the current black-out periods mandated by German law. The areas included in the database are some of Germany's largest and most historic cities (Berlin, Dresden, Mannheim, and Mainz, for example), as well as districts in both western and eastern Germany, ranging from Bavaria to the Palatinate to Lower Saxony to Pomerania. You can search for these individual databases by using the Ancestry.com Card Catalog.

Other Databases and Shared Assets

Ancestry.com has other collections of records that don't fit into a neat category, but it's still important to know what to expect from these databases and where they come from. Over the years, Ancestry.com has added searchable scans of many "core collection" books as databases, including such standards as *Pennsylvania German Pioneers*, edited by Ralph B. Strassburger and William J. Hinke (Pennsylvania German Society, 1934)—though, interestingly, it breaks the books of this two-volume publication into separate databases.

Some databases, especially those Ancestry.com added years ago, do not include scans of the original books and therefore can only be name searched. These collections have undergone optical character recognition, or OCR, which makes them keyword searchable. For example, while *Pennsylvania German Pioneers* includes a scanned copy of the original book (image **B**), other resources like New Jersey German Reformed Church Records, 1763–1802 **<search.ancestry.com/search/db.aspx?dbid=3315>**, which was originally published in print form, only has an OCR version (image **C**).

Of course, other major record groups—such as the US census and the National Archives Passenger Arrival Lists—are no longer unique to Ancestry.com but are standards for research no matter what a person's ethnicity is. Record groups like these are covered in more detail in the *Unofficial Guide to Ancestry.com*.

PUBLIC MEMBER TREES

In addition to looking directly for records on Ancestry.com, you can also take advantage of other users' work. Many users make their family trees publicly available on the site to share their research with others. Public member trees that have been compiled by Ancestry.com members have good qualities, too: Many have been made, and as Ancestry.com makes

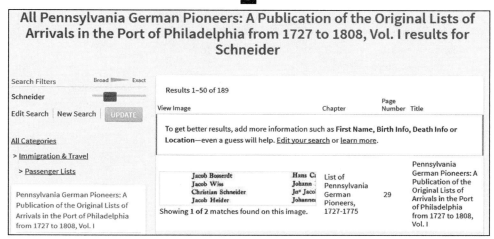

Having imaged records allows you to survey the original document for contextual information or botched transcriptions.

Some collections on Ancestry.com are indexed but do not have images of the original record. While indexed records can be keyword searched, you may miss out on important information by viewing records without their accompanying images.

its interfaces more sophisticated, users have better and better ways to add bibliographic sources to the individuals on their trees and link to the actual records.

Of course, making such tools available and having members actually use them are two different things. Remember that phrase "huge echo chamber of unverified information" from chapter 2? Well, that's true here as well. No Ancestry.com users have to qualify their information when creating public member trees, and so you should always verify information you find here before adding it to your own research.

The benefit of this setup is less stress for users of Ancestry.com's family trees than users of FamilySearch's Family Tree might experience, as Ancestry.com will not attempt to merge individuals' profiles, and other members can't edit your Ancestry.com family tree. While this prevents genealogical range wars between two researchers with different views about what records relate to a particular individual, this leaves a large pool of flotsam and jetsam bobbling around: references to what appears to be the same individual duplicated in many family trees from the same tenuous or even nonexistent information.

But once again, this is not a recommendation to avoid using the public member trees on Ancestry.com, only an admonition to use them carefully. They provide potential research clues that can be invaluable time savers.

OTHER ARMS OF ANCESTRY.COM

Of course, the folks behind Ancestry.com own many other properties. Some of these other arms are separate subscription services (such as Newspapers.com and Fold3) while others are essentially nonprofit properties that Ancestry has bought and continued to prop up (such as RootsWeb and Find A Grave <www.findagrave.com>). As usual, you can look to the *Unofficial Guide to Ancestry.com* for more details on some of the other sites and businesses in the Ancestry.com portfolio. We should point out some features of the sister sites that will be useful to the German genealogist.

Perhaps the most notable offshoot of Ancestry.com is AncestryDNA, one of the few companies that offers genealogically useful DNA testing. Going into the details of DNA is beyond this book's scope, but the general concept is that when significant portions of two individuals' DNA overlap, it indicates some sort of relationship between the two people. Genealogical brick walls can come tumbling down when this overlapping DNA between two or more people is combined with the paper documentation of the individuals. While DNA projects can also reveal that someone's legal father wasn't really his genetic father, these projects can also help the participants ferret out changes in spellings of surnames. For example, a descendant with the name *Grass* whose ancestor was thought to use that name (or *Gross* instead) found herself genetically related to Kress families in Germany.

Newspapers.com and Fold3 are two other arms of Ancestry.com, though they'll cost you extra if you don't have an All Access membership with Ancestry.com. Newspapers.com is exactly as its name implies—a collection of digitized, searchable historical newspapers from all across America. While the service has not emphasized acquiring German-language newspapers, it does have some of them that were included with other, larger collections. Unfortunately, there's no way to search just for German-language newspapers, but you can drill down from the nearly four thousand titles that Newspapers.com has in its portfolio by going to its All Newspapers page **<www.newspapers.com/papers>** and using the tools on the left side of the page to narrow the list. You could, for example, search for a newspaper by name and include the German articles for the—*Der, Die, Das*—and other words typically used in German newspaper titles (*Tägelich* for "daily," *Wochen-* for "weekly", etc.).

Fold3, on the other hand, specializes in American military records, and one of its hallmarks is allowing users to annotate records when they have more information about individuals who are mentioned. Fold3 has digital copies of the full Revolutionary War pension files, which sometimes contain detailed information in the affidavits files by the former soldiers seeking benefits.

RootsWeb was the first genealogy megasite and remains free to users since its acquisition by Ancestry.com. Here, you'll find oodles of family message boards as well as the impromptu home pages for some local genealogy groups and family associations that don't have their own websites. RootsWeb, too, has many educational articles as well as various databases. You can find a directory of them on the German RootsWeb landing page **<www.rootsweb.ancestry.com/~wggerman>**. One resource of interest to German researchers is a gazetteer of Alsace, an area that is currently French but was historically German **<www.rootsweb.ancestry.com/~fraalsac/alsaceaz/geninfoeng.htm>**.

TIPS, CAVEATS, AND FORECASTS

Ancestry.com says, "Acquiring German records is a large focus for Ancestry at this time," and there's no doubt the company means it. Ancestry.com is pursuing deals with German archives and continuing its partnership with FamilySearch.org. Ancestry.com's expertise has won it contracts around the world, including those giving the site more American records in categories that may help German genealogists find references to ancestors' European hometowns.

Ancestry.com has also shown a willingness to "do things right" in its quest for data. For example, when nearly half a century of Pennsylvania's death certificates became available for scanning in one fell swoop, Ancestry.com agreed to scan the original certificates for the best digital appearance rather than taking the easy way out and scanning from the state health department's microfilms of questionable quality.

A trend just beginning to crest at Ancestry.com is expanding user-provided material, something that has been more of a hallmark of its competitor MyHeritage <**www.myheritage.com**>. With the new LifeStory and Media Gallery function on its family trees, Ancestry.com is encouraging its members and subscribers to post trees, photos, mementos, and family records, possibly to create a larger and more engaged subscriber base.

Changing the emphasis of family trees in an attempt to get more subscribers is good business, and claiming that Ancestry.com's focus on family trees (many of which don't have to be sourced and so are easily snapped) isn't quite fair. Rather, the site should be applauded for providing the tools—such as better ways to integrate sources into the pages of the people on the public trees—and really can't be criticized when people don't use those tools.

The bottom line is that anyone with a continuing interest in German genealogy will be rewarded for having an Ancestry.com subscription. It's a place to plant your family tree amidst many of the records and sources, and to help you extend that tree beyond the Atlantic Ocean, perhaps for generations. And with AncestryDNA, the site has the potential to break down brick walls created by incomplete paper trails as well as give insights into a person's ancient pedigree.

KEYS TO SUCCESS

- If you're unsure of whether you want to pay for an Ancestry.com subscription, take advantage of free items available to nonsubscribing Ancestry Members, such as the *Meyers Gazetteer*.

- Begin your ancestor research on Ancestry.com by searching the site's main generic search form, but know that you'll still want to search individual databases so relevant results don't get lost in the shuffle.

- Identify specific databases to search by using Ancestry.com's Card Catalog. In addition to the *Meyers Gazetteer*, important collections for German researchers include the Hamburg Embarkation Lists and their indexes, plus ethnic German church registers and a growing number of German civil registers.

- Mine the other arms of Ancestry.com for features useful to German genealogists: Public Member Trees, AncestryDNA, and fellow member sites like Newspapers.com, Fold3, and RootsWeb.

ANCESTRY.COM IMMIGRATION RESOURCES AT A GLANCE

Some of the German records on Ancestry.com are more applicable to one or the other of the two major waves of immigrants: the "first boat" of those who came in Colonial times through the early Federal period (1600s through 1800) or those of the "second boat" who came in the nineteenth and early-twentieth centuries. Of course, both types of records will apply in some cases.

Here is a chart of some of the unique German resources on Ancestry.com and to which group they apply more readily:

	First Wave (1600s–1800)	Second Wave (1800–1930s)
Pennsylvania German Pioneers	x	
Rupp's 30,000 Names	x	
Germans to America		x
Passenger Arrival Lists		x
Hamburg Embarkation Lists		x
German state censuses	x	x
German church records	x	x *(secondary to civil registration)*
Historical Society of Pennsylvania Church and Town records	x	x
Evangelical Lutheran records		x
German Civil Registrations		x
Naturalizations	x *(colonies)*	x *(states and federal)*
Meyers Gazetteer	x	x
US census		x
Emigration databases		x *(primarily)*

6

GENEALOGY.NET: TWO WEBSITES IN ONE

've always been interested in maps and geography, and when I began doing genealogy, that affection of mine only grew stronger. Back in predigital days, I used a series of books titled *The Atlantic Bridge to Germany* (Everton, 1978) with maps and village names for each part of modern Germany in my research. Then I was introduced to *Meyer's Gazetteer of the German Empire* (and later cheered when Ancestry.com made it a free item **<search.ancestry.com/search/db.aspx?dbid=1074>**). And I was wowed when the University of Wisconsin put Ravenstein's atlas online **<uwdc.library.wisc.edu/collections/German/Ravenstein>**. I also bought a German road atlas or two. But while all these tools were helpful, nothing compared to a the huge village dictionary called GOV (*Genealogische Ortsverzeichnis*) and its more than one million entries that were put online by the German site Genealogy.net **<www.compgen.de>**.

We'll come back to GOV, but I've mentioned it here because it's one of the prime resources on the German supersite run by the Verein für Computergenealogie e.V. (the Association for Computer Genealogy; the *e.V.* stands for *eingetragener Verein*, which translates as "registered association"). One thing that's difficult when it comes to this

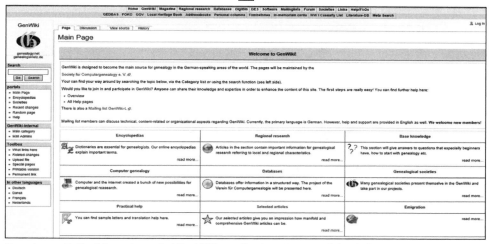

Genealogy.net's English version, called GenWiki, can direct you to some of the site's sources.

massive site: deciding how to refer to it, since the URLs *Genealogy.net*, *Compgen.de*, and *Genealogienetz.de* all link to the default German version of the site. And as if that weren't enough, the English version of the site goes by GenWiki **<wiki-en.genealogy.net>**. For our purposes, we'll simply call the site *"Genealogy.net"* when talking about the German language features (and any of those three domain names listed earlier) and *GenWiki* only when referring to the parts translated into English.

As compared to the many-armed "octopus" sites FamilySearch.org **<www.familysearch. org>** and Ancestry.com **<www.ancestry.com>**, Genealogy.net is much less centralized. Rather, we can fairly call Genealogy.net a consortium of Web portals that can be challenging to understand, made more difficult by the fact that most of this site's material appears only in German. But this free site (content is available to all users, but a no-cost registration allows the several additional privileges detailed in this chapter) has so many facets that you'll want to mine the background information and databases in both languages.

ARCHITECTURE OF THE ENGLISH VERSION

GenWiki touts that its mission is "to become the main source for genealogy in the German-speaking areas of the world." When all its German-language resources are totaled up, the site has a good claim toward fulfilling its mission, and the English version of the site does have many important features. But unlike most websites that have an English version, the German version doesn't allow you to click through to get to the English version of the site—you'll need to use the GenWiki URL listed earlier.

Genealogy.net at a Glance

Most folks have heard of Ancestry.com and FamilySearch.org, but fewer know the features and uses of Genealogy.net. Here's a review of all the major parts of GenWiki/Genealogy. net for when you take the site for a test drive. Begin with the English side (unless you're fluent in German):

GenWiki <wiki-en.genealogy.net/Main_Page>

- Look at the FAQ, which gives profiles of some features that are found on the German side. Test out Transserv, which provides a human translation.
- Skim through the genealogical associations/societies that host their websites on GenWiki.
- Run your ancestors through the Meta Search, remembering that not all databases respond with the short time frame mandated, so you might need to complete individual searches.
- Explore GOV, the genealogy gazetteer for help locating villages.

Genealogy.net <compgen.de>

- Use the Forum to ask questions.
- Skim through the additional Vereine (Associations or Societies) pages on the German side for groups in your geographic area of research.
- Use Regional Research **<wiki-de.genealogy.net/Portal:Regionale_Forschung>** for details and background information on particular areas of German-speaking areas of Europe.
- Look through DigiBib **<wiki-de.genealogy.net/Portal:DigiBib>**, the collection of digitized out-of-copyright historic books.
- Search the GEDBAS family trees **<gedbas.genealogy.net>** and perhaps upload one of your own.
- Utilize FOKO's searchable database of queries.
- Leaf through the Ortsfamilienbücher, which compile all the families from a particular village.
- Examine the Adressbücher if a city of ancestry is included.

Entering *wiki-en.genealogy.net/Main_Page* in your browser's URL bar brings you to the English version's main page (image **A**). The site is then sorted into ten portals, some of which are incomplete and others that turn into German immediately upon being clicked. As noted previously, you don't particularly need to create a login at the get-go and won't need an account to access the information and databases. Registration is only needed to generate your own content; for example, you need a login to upload a family tree in GEDBAS (profiled later in the German-language section of this chapter) or to edit GenWiki articles.

STEP-BY-STEP EXAMPLE: CREATING AN ACCOUNT ON GENWIKI

1 Go to **<wiki-en.genealogy.net/Main_Page>** and click Log in at upper-right corner of the page.

2 On the Log in/create account screen, scroll down and click a bolded statement that reads "follow this link."

3

> **Request an account**
>
> Thank you for your interest in our genealogical databases. You will only need an account, if you wish to put your own genealogical data into our databases. If you wish to perform only searches in our databases, you do not need to fillout the following form. In this case, just go back to the query page of the specific database.
>
> If you are already a member of one german genealogical society using an "online membership database on genealogy.net", you can use your account from that society and do not to fill out the following form and can go directly to the database **login** screen (left menu on this page).
>
> If you still want to get an account, please fill out the following form and hit "Request account". One of our admins will take care on your request and send an e-mail to you, when your account is activated.
>
> **1. User-Data** (* = mandatory)
>
> * Account name:
>
> * Password :
>
> * Password (type in again):
>
> **Please remember your chosen account name and password.**
> Both are used for login after you receive an e-mail which tells you that your account is activated.

3 Fill in the required information: account name (the username you select), a password, "prename" (first name), surname, e-mail address, country, and address. In addition, check the box signifying that you have read and agreed to the privacy statements, then hit Request account. Note the click-through to the privacy statements comes up in German, but you can use Google Translate **<translate.google.com>** to get an English version. You'll receive an e-mail acceptance of your login. You can click a box allowing you to stay logged in.

The Basics

If you choose to register for the site, your username will show up on the top right-hand side of the page. The English GenWiki Main Page gives you a menu of ten items and also has several lists on the left-hand side that repeat some of the entries from the menu of portals, plus a list of help features, some of which immediately default to the German language upon being clicked.

The Encyclopedias, Computer genealogy, and Practical help portals are all fairly skeletal on GenWiki, but the Base knowledge portal has an excellent Frequently Asked Questions (FAQ), not just for the site but also one that goes into a lot of the basics of German genealogy. In addition, Base knowledge also has English-language descriptions of some of the prime assets that appear on the German side of the site. While other selections from the English-side menu are either blank (Selected Articles) or barely started (Emigration and Miscellaneous), the Regional Research tab is a fertile portal—but it turns into German right away, so we'll discuss the more robust features of the German side in further detail. You'll find that Google Translate will truly be your friend on this site, page after page.

Genealogical Societies

The GenWiki/Genealogy.net site provides much the same role for German genealogy societies as the RootsWeb site now owned by Ancestry.com does for American societies; the German megasite provides Web pages for more than thirty associations based in Europe. Most of these societies have a starter page on the English side, but in most cases, you'll want to go to the German side for more complete information about these organizations.

Databases

This portal is the gateway for a number of interesting and useful databases, including a shortcut to look at those with personal name information through the all-at-once Meta Search (image **B**). This function searches about a dozen large databases affiliated with the site, including some that we'll profile in more detail on the German-language side. The caveat with Meta Search is that it only lists results that come back very quickly, so this is a quick-and-dirty search that might need to be repeated with the individual databases. Nevertheless, it's a good starting point that encompasses searches of the family tree (GEDBAS) and query (FOKO) databases.

B

Start new search

genealogy.net Meta Search will send requests to all databases simultaneously and will wait 10 seconds for responses. As with first database response search results will be shown - while search in the other databases is going on in the background until 10 seconds are exhausted.

last name:

place name:

Start search

Metasearch does requests in databases:

☑ GEDBAS
☑ Datenbank Historischer Adressbücher
☑ FOKO
☑ Forschungsdatenbanken der Vereine
☑ Online Ortsfamilienbücher
☑ Volkszahlregister Schleswig Holstein (AGGSH e. V.)
☑ Grabsteine
☑ Verlustlisten 1. Weltkrieg
☑ Grabsteine Ostfriesland (Upstalsboom-Gesellschaft e. V.)
☑ Sterbebilder (Bayerischer Landesverein für Familienkunde e.V.)
Bremer Passagierlisten (passagierlisten.de)

Genealogy.net's Meta Search will comb through all of the site's databases at once. Its broad scope, however, may result in your missing some records.

The million-place-strong *Genealogische Ortsverzeichnis* ("genealogical gazetteer," also known as GOV) is a great go-to item on this site since it is constantly being expanded and includes not just Germany but also other once-German areas of Europe (and, increasingly, some nonGerman localities, too). One of the many reasons to search GOV is that it picks up historical villages that may have been merged out of existence, too.

STEP-BY-STEP EXAMPLE: SEARCHING THE GOV

1 Click the Databases portal on GenWiki **<wiki-en.genealogy.net/Main_Page>**. From the resulting menu, click GOV—German locations.

2 On the Historic Gazetteer page, fill in the search box with a name (such as *Mauchenheim*). You also have the alternative of Extended search; click on it, and you'll get more sophisticated searching parameters, such as being able to find two places at once.

3 View your results. Searching *Mauchenheim* resulted in a map of the four closest-matching results. In this case, three of the four relate to one particular village. You can click on the individual results for more information on each.

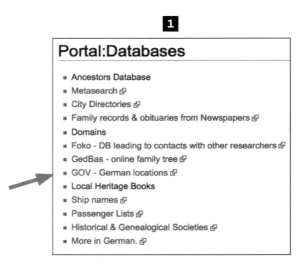

Portal:Databases

- Ancestors Database
- Metasearch
- City Directories
- Family records & obituaries from Newspapers
- Domains
- Foko - DB leading to contacts with other researchers
- GedBas - online family tree
- GOV - German locations
- Local Heritage Books
- Ship names
- Passenger Lists
- Historical & Genealogical Societies
- More in German.

2

The Historic Gazetteer

Place name: [_____]

[Search]

Extended search

The precise identification of places is essential in genealogy. Unfortunately, too few researchers care in identifying places. The project "GOV" was initiated to help historians and genealogists with the management of place references and to provide high quality data for anyone.

Over time GOV will evolve into a valuable resource for genealogists, historians and sociologists that allows unified access to a variety of location-based data, and in particular to the facts that are relevant to the work of genealogists:

- Geographical location of the place (coordinates or a position on a map)
- Several properties of a place (postal code, town-code, etc.)
- Foreign or former names
- Past affiliation (administrative, law, church, etc.)

GOV contains churches, church districts, places, districts, regions, etc.. Internally, an entry is commonly referred to as "GOV object".

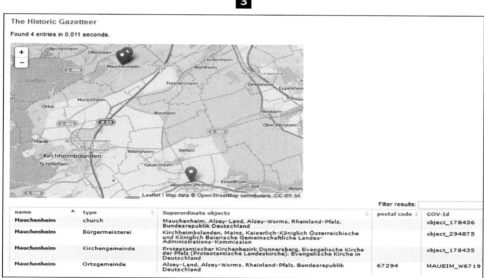

The Historic Gazetteer

Found 4 entries in 0.011 seconds.

Leaflet | Map data © OpenStreetMap contributors, CC-BY-SA

Filter results: [_____]

name	type	Superordinate objects	postal code	GOV-Id
Mauchenheim	church	Mauchenheim, Alzey-Land, Alzey-Worms, Rheinland-Pfalz, Bundesrepublik Deutschland		object_178436
Mauchenheim	Bürgermeisterei	Kirchheimbolanden, Mainz, Kaiserlich-Königlich Österreichische und Königlich Baierische Gemeinschaftliche Landes-Administrations-Kommission		object_294875
Mauchenheim	Kirchengemeinde	Protestantischer Kirchenbezirk Donnersberg, Evangelische Kirche der Pfalz (Protestantische Landeskirche), Evangelische Kirche in Deutschland		object_178435
Mauchenheim	Ortsgemeinde	Alzey-Land, Alzey-Worms, Rheinland-Pfalz, Bundesrepublik Deutschland	67294	MAUEIM_W6719

GERMAN-LANGUAGE INTERFACE AND EXTRAS

The German-language start page <www.compgen.de> (image **C**) lists the site's main features; keep this start page active on one window of your computer before feeding the page into Google Translate so you see the feature headings in German, too. The headings are divided into three sections: Informationen (Information), Datenbanken (Databases), and Weitere Angebote (More Offers). Here's a quick rundown of all the headings, in German (with their English translations as necessary); the more important parts of the portal will be detailed in separate sections.

Informationen contains valuable resources to help people make the most of the site and includes the following headings:

- GenWiki: This page mirrors the format of the English version, though many items (such as the lists of abbreviations and occupations) that are skeletal on the English side are fully filled in the German pages. Importantly, this page has a *Suche* (Search) function to seek out pages of the sprawling site that do not readily come up in other menus. For example, the *Deutsches Geschlechterbuch*, a multivolume set of family trees published in annual volumes beginning in 1889, can be found through this search, including digital pages of many volumes.

- News: Here you'll find updates on items added to the site.

- Regional: This leads to one of the gems of Genealogy.net—detailed pages on nearly all of Germany's states and regions with excellent background information on history and types of records available (more on this later).

- DigiBib (short for *Digitalen Bibliothek*, or "Digital Library"): Another Genealogy.net gem, DigiBib (also detailed later) is a collection of digitized out-of-copyright historic books and source material.

- DES (Data Entry System): Looking to add information to Genealogy.net? This page will show you how.

Verein für Computergenealogie e.V.

Willkommen auf dem deutschen Genealogieserver

Alles rund um Familienforschung (Ahnenforschung/Genealogie)

Der Verein für Computergenealogie e. V. betreibt mehrere Internetserver. Von dieser Portalseite aus können Sie direkt auf die verschiedenen Angebote zugreifen. Viele unserer Datenbanken können Sie über unsere Metasuche direkt "in einem Rutsch" abfragen.

Informationen

GenWiki	Hauptsammlung unserer Informationsseiten
News	Monatliche Neuigkeiten (Rundbrief)
Regional	Finden Sie Forschungshilfen in vielen Regionen
DigiBib	Digitalisierte Ausgaben historischer Bücher und Quellen
DES	Unser Datenerfassungssystem für digitalisatierte genealogische Quellen jeder Art
Software	Informationen über Genealogieprogramme
Mailinglisten	Mehr als 100 Mailinglisten in denen sich Forscher austauschen
Forum	Das größte und aktivste deutschsprachige Forum für Familienforscher
Vereine	Homepages von mehr als 35 genealogischen Vereinen
Hilfen/FAQs	Wie fange ich mit der Familienforschung an?

Datenbanken

Gedbas	Komplette Ahnenlisten/Stammbäume durchsuchen und bereitstellen
FOKO	Die Aktion "Forscherkontakte" der DAGV
GOV	Genealogisches Ortsverzeichnis
Ortsfamilienbücher	Komplette Ortsfamilienbücher sind online abfragbar
Adressbücher	Informationen aus historischen Adressbüchern
Familienanzeigen	Familienanzeigen aus Tageszeitungen
Grabsteine	Online Dokumentation von Grabsteinen auf Friedhöfen
Totenzettel	Daten aus Totenzettelsammlungen
Verlustlisten	Datenbank der Verlustlisten des 1. Weltkrieges
Literaturdatenbank	Die "Familiengeschichtliche Bibliografie" der DAGV

Weitere Angebote

RSS-Feeds	Attraktive Inhalte für Ihre Homepage
Lexika	Krankheits- und Berufsbezeichnungen, Vor- und Familiennamen, etc.
Kalender	Ausstellungen, Treffen, Vorträge und mehr für Familienforscher
Kontakt	vorstand@compgen.de

You'll find most of Genealogy.net's resources on the German side of the site. Knowing a bit of German and using translation software like Google Translate will go a long way in aiding your research.

- Software: Learn about different genealogy software programs, including Family Tree Maker and Familienbuch, two family-tree-making programs.

- Mailinglisten (Mailing Lists): This page contains more than a hundred lists that researchers can subscribe to.

- Forum: Ask questions and create threads about genealogy topics here.

- Vereine (Associations or Societies): Genealogy groups that have pages on the English side—and additional organizations that don't, totaling about three-dozen in all—host their websites here.

- Hilfen/FAQs ("Help" and "Frequently Asked Questions"): Need some help about where to start? Check out these help topics.

Arguably the most important part of the site, Datenbanken connects users to the site's collections of records and is made up of these headings:

- GEDBAS (a clipped form of "GEDCOM database"): Family trees that users have contributed live here (and are detailed later).

- FOKO (short for *Forscherkontakte*, "Researcher Contacts"): Search this database of queries if you need to contact professional researchers for information—more on this later.

- GOV, the *Genealogisches Ortsverzeichnis*: As has been discussed in the section on the English side of the site, this valuable resource contains the names of towns and villages that may no longer exist.

- Ortsfamilienbücher (Local Heritage Books): These books, which compile all the families from a particular village, are available here in a searchable database. We'll discuss these in more detail later in this chapter and in chapter 9.

- Adressbücher (City Directories): These resources are collections of year-by-year residential lists from urban areas—more on these later.

- Familienanzeigen (Family Notices): These include personal notes taken from newspapers, including birth and wedding announcements and other notices such as graduations.

- Grabsteine (Gravestones): While many physical gravestones have been removed (see chapter 1), records of them survive in databases like this one.

- Totenzettel (Funeral Notices): A deceased person's biography was often presented at his funeral service, and these sources can be found here.

- Verlustlisten (Casualty Lists): This ongoing project documents those who were killed, wounded, or missing in World War I.

- Literaturdatenbank (Literature Database): Here, you can search list of articles published in various genealogy journals.

Finally, Weitere Angebote contains some miscellaneous features that German researchers may find helpful when using the site. Its subheadings include:

- RSS Feeds: Receive automatic updates about certain parts of the website using this feature.

- Lexika (Encyclopedias): Having trouble with vocabulary? Check out this section's lists of words about diseases, occupations, weights and measures, and more, many of them archaic and therefore used in old documents.

- Kalender (Calendar): As you might expect, you can view upcoming events related to genealogy here, including TV shows and events hosted by genealogical societies.

- Kontakt (Contact): Here, you'll find the site's e-mail address as well as the e-mail addresses of its executive board and key people.

Regional Research

The Regional Research page <wiki-de.genealogy.net/Portal:Regionale_Forschung> is among the richest features of Genealogy.net. For most every part of Germany, past and present (as well as places in Eastern Europe in which there were German-speaking enclaves), you can find historical articles, help with present-day places, and previous political divisions of the German states and overviews of record groups that are available. The Regional Research page itself is divided into a menu of several choices, the most helpful of which are the Regionale Themenportale (Regional Thematic Portals), which are divided mostly by present-day German states, including Bavaria, Hesse, Prussia, the Palatinate, and Württemberg.

DigiBib (Digital Library)

DigiBib, which is an abbreviation for *Digitalen Bibliothek* (meaning simply "Digital Library") <wiki-de.genealogy.net/Portal:DigiBib>, has a growing cache of printed material that has been digitized and is being OCR or typed out by volunteers for easier use, although the digitized originals remain accessible, too. Because some of the books have not been made searchable, you might need to just look at titles, then choose the digitized pages to scrutinize for yourself.

GEDBAS (GEDCOM Database)

Genealogy.net's version of public family trees is called *GEDBAS* <gedbas.genealogy.net>. Unlike the type of trees that FamilySearch.org, Ancestry.com, and MyHeritage promote,

GEDBAS has no function for directly creating your family tree on the Genealogy.net site. Instead, users are encouraged to upload a GEDCOM file, which is the standard format for family tree information used by many software programs for ease of transfer. Typically, you'll search this database for an individual's name (or just a surname), and once you get a hit in a particular family tree, you have the option of showing all persons from that particular file so you can look at the whole tree, and contributors are identified so they can establish contact and exchange search results.

FOKO (Researcher Contacts)

FOKO is a database of names, particularly surnames, that shows how to get more information on that name from an individual or institution. The site contains more than a million and half names represented on FOKO, an average of ten results per surname. Note that FOKO will switch back to German after a few screens, even if you're in Google Translate. Because of this, you'll need to call up a separate Google Translate text box and cut-and-paste the German words into it for a translation (though again, as pointed out earlier in this book, these translations aren't foolproof).

Ortsfamilienbücher (Local Heritage Books)

These books are a ticket to research heaven when you find one for the village of your ancestor. You'll find more details about the clever way these books are organized by the ever-efficient Germans in chapter 9, since databases outside Genealogy.net have collections of these books.

But for now, know that these books are ordinarily compiled by an expert local historian or genealogist who has sorted together all the families found in a particular locality from the beginning of the community's records. Genealogy.net has extracted several hundred of these books and made them searchable, first by a particular individual's name, then by showing that person in the context of his or her family.

Adressbücher (City Directories)

Genealogy.net has a large collection of digitized and mostly searchable city directories from German cities. The collection contains more than two thousand such volumes, though with multiple annual volumes for many of the cities, the collection represents only a few hundred actual places. Some of this collection overlaps with records that FamilySearch.org has online.

TIPS, CAVEATS, AND FORECASTS

In chapters 2 and 3, you were given your marching orders (gently and perhaps subtly) to learn some German as a way of helping discover the maximum number of German genealogy resources, and hopefully you've taken that direction to heart. Genealogy.net is where this comes home to roost since, as you've seen in this chapter, the English side of GenWiki has a lot less to offer than the German side. When you travel to Germany in person, the great majority of Germans are friendly and accommodating of Americans who don't speak any German (though they are friendlier if you know a little and at least try to start the conversation in their language). The vibe on this Internet site, however, is a little different; let's face it, German speakers have every right to take the attitude, "This is a German website, and anything we give you in English is a bonus."

When answering a question about enhancements to the English version, a representative of the site responded that "there are certainly plans to expand it in the future, but there is no concrete road map." Which is another way of saying, "It's not a priority, so we'll get to it when we get to it." It's important to remember that Genealogy.net and its sister site GenWiki are volunteer efforts, and the wiki format allows anyone with interest to make edits; the site really needs more English-speaking volunteers to take the time to add content. (Once you've registered, feel free to go at it!) But despite the "if and when" nature of all things wiki, the bottom line is that this site's German-language side has exceptional background resources, helpful databases, and good communication tools. All German genealogists wanting a thorough search for their ancestors need to spend time on the site.

KEYS TO SUCCESS

- Use your German language skills (or Google Translate) to work with the German side of Genealogy.net. While the English version of the site is a good starting point, a huge amount of information is found only in German.

- Search individual databases separately, as the Meta Search only brings back quick results and may miss some resources.

- Take advantage of the site's most valuable asset: the GOV gazetteer, which can help you find villages throughout German-speaking Europe.

- Broaden your research to include the other marquee items at Genealogy.net, such as regional background pages, public family trees (GEDBAS), an inquiry service (FOKO), a large database of search results from local heritage books, and more.

7

MYHERITAGE: A FOREST OF FAMILY TREES

When you've been doing genealogy for more than thirty years (and when half of that time has been as a professional genealogist), the gaps in your own personal tree are likely to be the most stubborn of problems. One of those frustrating roadblocks came tumbling down a couple of years ago when my home state of Pennsylvania turned its older death certificates over to public records, eventually resulting in online access to these records. Such easy access allowed me to quickly pull the death certificates of siblings of my direct-line ancestors, some of which had more information on parents' names than my particular great-great-great-grandfather's certificate. As a consequence, I was able to add *Heberling* to my list of ancestral surnames.

But trying to find information about the Heberling immigrant, who appeared to be a German or Swiss man named Rudolph was, well, trying—that is, until I did a Google search, where the only helpful hit directed me to one of the millions of family trees on MyHeritage <www.myheritage.com>. The person who had entered that particular tree stated that Rudolph was of Swiss origin (without any sources, of course, so I took that with a grain of salt), but what really got my attention was that it showed his immigrant arrival specifically on the ship *Isaac* on September 27, 1749, at the port of Philadelphia.

Now this was something I could check out in the *Pennsylvania German Pioneers* by Ralph B. Strassburger and William J. Hinke (Pennsylvania German Society, 1934); of course, I had previously checked that book's index to no avail. But what I found was a man making an *X* for his signature, by which the captain or a fellow passenger had written *Rutolph Haberly*, a spelling corruption that hadn't occurred to me. In an instant, this family was no longer "trying" to me.

This example of success demonstrates that a critical mass of websites with large numbers of searchable family trees will inevitably be of some use to you. And "large numbers of family trees" is a specialty—perhaps the top specialty—of the internationally based MyHeritage enterprise. As we'll see, MyHeritage also has searchable databases of records and some substantial bells and whistles to its searching algorithms that can especially benefit beginning genealogists looking for quick finds.

FAMILY TREES ON MYHERITAGE

As befits the site's name, MyHeritage has more of a worldwide membership base than perhaps any other single genealogy group. As a consequence, MyHeritage is offered in nearly four dozen different languages. This can be particularly useful when families from different parts of the globe collaborate on a single family tree. MyHeritage has some eighty million registered users, including about three million Germans. The site's users have compiled close to thirty million family trees, and that figure doesn't even include

A

The MyHeritage home page is your gateway to accessing the site's many features.

B

Family tree	Disc...
Family tree	
People	
Relationship report	
Sources	
Manage trees	
Import GEDCOM	
Backup	
Print charts & books	

Family trees are MyHeritage's most prominent feature.

POWER-USER TIP

Put It on the Map
When researching in some databases that return locations as part of the textual research result, click on the place name to view with a map showing that place. This feature is a convenient shortcut to see where that village is located (though sometimes it picks up the name of the village's district and displays it instead of the actual village).

those from the completely free MyHeritage affiliate Geni **<www.geni.com>**, where millions more have uploaded their pedigree information.

MyHeritage offers users a limited amount of family tree space with some functionality for free and owns the Family Tree Builder software. Looking at its record databases requires one of a few different subscription plans, which include Premium and Premium Plus. While you can create a relatively small family tree for free, paid subscription is also required depending on the volume of family tree information stored on the site. Many genealogical societies provide a discount on membership, so seek out those deals to make the best use of your money.

Your home page (image **A**) will vary once you've set up a family tree, but the primary tabs at the top will stay same. Hovering on the Family tree tab will bring up a list of options. Choose Family tree on the top of the list (image **B**). Next you'll see a form to put in a person's name and dates—fill that in, and you're off and running.

Searching and Matching Capabilities

MyHeritage has several specialized searching technologies that can help users build a family tree and search through others' quickly. For people who are literally just beginning a family tree online, MyHeritage offers the Instant Discoveries function, in which a user new to MyHeritage is asked to enter basic information about himself and his parents and grandparents to receive on-the-spot discoveries, kind of a genealogy speed dating experience. MyHeritage says it tries to minimize false positives but, of course,

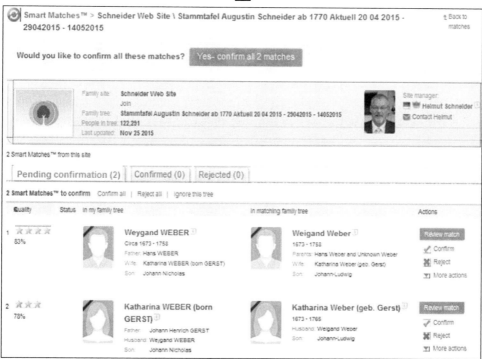

MyHeritage's Smart Match, like Ancestry.com's "shaky leaves," allows users to compare their ancestor's profile to profiles from other users' family trees and attach relevant information.

identifying false positives partially rests on the skills of the new user, who is likely to be an inexperienced researcher.

Once a person has created a family tree on MyHeritage, she can use the Smart Matching process (image C), which takes individuals on your tree and compares them to millions of trees created by other MyHeritage users around the world in the same order as the shaking leaves at Ancestry.com. MyHeritage presents potential matches with a percentage score, indicating how closely its search algorithms say the results match. You can then confirm or reject if the two entries are the same person. The Record Matches technology works somewhat similarly but comes from records discovered in SuperSearch, automatically including a summary of additional records and individuals in family trees relating to it.

The site also has a Record Detective technology that attempts to use any single record found in SuperSearch to list additional records and individuals in family trees that may generate new leads and discoveries. Finally, Global Name Translation attempts to make adjustments for names (as well as nicknames) in different languages and alphabets, feeding back results not just in the language entered by the user. You can use a box (checked by default) on the SuperSearch form called With translations to activate this technology.

GERMAN DATABASES

Once you get past the huge number of family trees on MyHeritage, the exclusive offerings of records are somewhat modest. You can view the site's databases related to Germany at **<www.myheritage.com/research/category-Germany/germany?sac=1>**.

Its biggest databases (German births, marriages, and deaths) will look strikingly familiar if you've read this book, because they are the same databases that were compiled by FamilySearch.org and shared with Ancestry.com (and, just like Ancestry.com, MyHeritage uses the threefold-higher number of "records" to inflate the count). In addition, data from FamilySearch Family Trees also shows up in MyHeritage search results.

MyHeritage does have a large database of West Prussia Church Books that appears to be unique, but the problem here is one of sourcing. The database description is vague on whether these are extractions straight from the church registers or whether (as is found in some parts of Germany) those registers have already been extracted previously. In the latter case, you might need to be on the lookout for transcription errors made when abstracts of the records were created from the extracts.

Other resources include volumes from printed genealogy compilations and periodicals such as the journal *Gothaisches Genealogisches Taschenbuch Der Freiherrlichen Häuser*, the four volumes of *Schlegel's American Families of German Ancestry in the United States*, and the publications of the Pennsylvania German Society. Like Genealogy.net, it has many volumes of the compiled genealogy series *Deutsches Geschlechterbuch*.

Despite having images of the originals attached, some databases can only be searched instead of browsed. And a fair number of the resources don't have images at all, just a list of textual search results. For example, the West Prussia Church Books database has no way to drill down to individual villages and then browse records from just that village (though of course the village name shows as part of the text result).

STEP-BY-STEP EXAMPLE: USING SUPERSEARCH TO FIND RECORDS

1 On the home page, hover over the Research tab to bring up a menu of choices. Click Search all records to bring up the SuperSearch form.

2 On the SuperSearch form, enter information about the ancestor or place you're looking for. Note that the site features a Calculate dropdown that can generate a potential birth year for your ancestor based on what age he was in a particular year.

3 Use the Categories menu to drill down to specific databases. This will help you narrow your results, though filtering too many categories may exclude potential finds.

1

Apps	Research
Search all records	
Birth, Marriage & Death	
Census & Voter Lists	
Family Trees	
Newspapers	
Immigration & Travel	
Hire a researcher	
DNA tests	

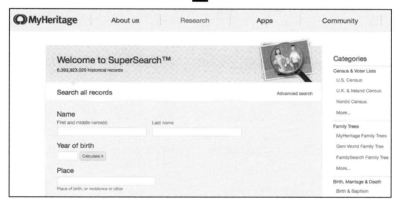

2

MyHeritage   About us   Research   Apps   Community

Welcome to SuperSearch™
6,393,923,029 historical records

Search all records   Advanced search

Name
First and middle name(s)   Last name

Year of birth
                Calculate it

Place

Place of birth, or residence or other

Categories

Census & Voter Lists
U.S. Census
U.K. & Ireland Census
Nordic Census
More...

Family Trees
MyHeritage Family Trees
Geni World Family Tree
FamilySearch Family Tree
More...

Birth, Marriage & Death
Birth & Baptism

3

Categories

Census & Voter Lists
U.S. Census
U.K. & Ireland Census
Nordic Census
More...

Family Trees
MyHeritage Family Trees
Geni World Family Tree
FamilySearch Family Tree
More...

TIPS, CAVEATS, AND FORECASTS

The future of MyHeritage promises more of its already established strengths: its global reach and its technological savvy. The service helps families "discover, preserve, and share their family history in an accessible and instantly rewarding way." MyHeritage's stated goal is to keep developing additional technologies that bring users and discoveries together with the least amount of muss and fuss.

In short, the story of MyHeritage is that the site was "first to the party" in leveraging what might be called the "family effect" of using public trees as the carrot to bring more people in each family into the site's fold. And while it's late to the party on digitizing actual records, MyHeritage is gamely attempting to make up for lost time. Where German records are concerned, it's true that, despite so many records that are online at one or another of the other major services, many German records (especially church and civil records) reside in backwater areas in Germany, still in local hands awaiting technology to descend upon them. MyHeritage's goal is to work even closer with the societies and organizations that are the custodians of these records in new partnerships.

KEYS TO SUCCESS

▢ Consider accessing the site for MyHeritage's vast number of searchable family trees and its selection of niche databases, some of which overlap with offerings at FamilySearch.org and Ancestry.com.

▢ Take advantage of MyHeritage's collection of millions of family trees from users around the world. Use its various search options to identify individuals and records that match your family tree.

8

ARCHION: PROTESTANT CHURCH RECORDS GALORE

The importance of church records in German genealogy can never be overstated. And the microfilms of German church records in the collections of FamilySearch's Family History Library system have long been one of the great assets for researchers outside of Germany. But despite the many villages included on these microfilms, many are not in that system for one reason or another.

For those with Protestant German ancestry, the church records megasite known as Archion <www.archion.de> (originally Kirchenbuchportal.de) has begun to fill that gap. Kirchenbuchportal GmbH (*Gesellschaft mit beschränkter Haftung*, or "company with limited liability," similar to a limited-liability company/LLC in the United States) was established in 2013 by a collection of Protestant churches (*Evangelische Kirche*). This entity, in turn, created the Archion website as the platform for the participating church bodies' digitized records.

The Archion site (image **A**) already has passed the five-million-page mark. While not all of the Protestant union's member churches are participating, an estimated 25 percent of church books from involved branches have been scanned. Those member churches pay for the ongoing digitization of their own records, and subscription payments by individual users pay the overall costs for the website.

Archion contains records from Protestant churches all over Germany.

KIRCHENBUCHPORTAL TO THE RESCUE

Archion has many valuable church records that can provide information you can't get anywhere else. Some of these are free upon registering for an account on the site, but many require a membership fee.

But before discussing what records are available, we should first identify which churches have contributed their holdings to the site. The full German names and coverage areas of the participating state church archives with registers already on Archion are listed here:

- Evangelisches Zentralarchiv in Berlin (Berlin, plus Prussia and many formerly German eastern areas)

- Landeskirchliches Archiv der Evangelisch-Lutherischen Kirche in Bayern (Bavaria)

- Landeskirchliches Archiv der Evangelischen Kirche von Westfalen (Westphalia)

- Landeskirchliches Archiv Hannover (Hannover)

- Evangelisches Landeskirchliches Archiv in Berlin (Berlin-Brandenburg-Silesian Oberlausitz)

- Landeskirchliches Archiv Karlsruhe (Baden)

- Landeskirchliches Archiv Kassel (Kurhessen-Waldeck; Electorate of Hesse and Waldeck)

- Landeskirchliches Archiv Stuttgart (Württemberg)

POWER-USER TIP

Beware the Borders
Note that the boundaries of the *Evangelisch* state churches do not follow the current *Land* boundaries; in some cases, they are leftover boundaries from the states of the old Second Reich.

- Zentralarchiv der Evangelischen Kirche der Pfalz (Palatinate)
- Zentralarchiv der Evangelischen Kirche in Hessen und Nassau (Hesse and Nassau)

Several partner churches that are involved in Archion have not yet posted digitized registers on the site. These include Anhalt, Nordkirche (Schleswig-Holstein, Mecklenburg, and Pomerania), Lippe (Lippe), and Braunschweig (Brunswick).

Appendix A contains a map showing the Protestant state churches participating in Archion. The Protestant churches that are not involved with Archion are mentioned in chapter 12.

What's Available for Free

You can investigate general information and search whether a particular church book has been digitized for free on Archion. In some cases, only a portion of the records of a particular parish or church district have been digitized and uploaded so far. Those in digital form are shown with a green background while those with a white background still exist only as originals or as microfilms. You can also look at the Forum for inquiries free of charge, but making a post on it requires that you create an account.

STEP-BY-STEP: SIGNING UP FOR ARCHION

1 Navigate to **<www.archion.de>** and click Registrieren.

1

2 Fill out the form: Vorname (first name), Nachname (last name), E-mail (e-mail address), Benutzername (desired username), and Land (country of residence). Check the box next to Datenschutzfreigabe to accept the terms and conditions for the site. Click Profil Jetzt Erstellen when you're finished. You will receive an e-mail with a temporary password. Navigate back to Archion to sign in for the first time.

3 Navigate back to Archion and click Login. Enter your user name in the Benutzername field and your password in the Passwort field. If you would like to remain logged in to Archion on this computer, check the Angemeldet Bleiben box. Click Anmelden to log in.

Buying Access on Archion

To look at the digital copies of the church registers or to download copies of pages from those registers, you'll need to purchase a "passport" that allows you to access a particular time period and a limited number of downloads. The site offers plans for "individuals" and "professionals," the latter being significantly more expensive but allowing for larger (but still limited) numbers of downloads as well as commercial use (image **B**). As of publication, Archion has three plans for "private" individuals, each with different time lengths and number of downloads allowed: thirty-days' access (fifty document downloads), twelve-months' access (six hundred downloads), and twenty-days' access measured by time logged in (fifty document downloads). Plans for "professionals" run at two to three times the price of the private plans but offer two to three times the number of

PAKET AUSWÄHLEN:

	1 Monat Privater Nutzer	1 Jahr Privater Nutzer	20 Tage (Kontingent) Privater Nutzer	1 Monat Professioneller Nutzer	1 Jahr Professioneller Nutzer	20 Tage (Kontingent) Professioneller Nutzer
Preis	19,90 € inkl. MwSt.	178,80 € inkl. MwSt.	59,90 € inkl. MwSt.	69,95 € inkl. MwSt.	599,00 € inkl. MwSt.	199,00 € inkl. MwSt.
Zeitraum	1 Monat	12 Monate	20 Tage (innerhalb 12 Monaten)	1 Monat	12 Monate	20 Tage (innerhalb 12 Monaten)
Nutzbarkeit	durchgehend	durchgehend	mit Unterbrechung	durchgehend	durchgehend	mit Unterbrechung
Downloads *	50	600	50	175	2000	175
	BUCHEN	BUCHEN	BUCHEN	BUCHEN	BUCHEN	BUCHEN

Archion offers a variety of paid subscription plans for both private individuals and professionals. You'll need a subscription to access many of the site's features.

downloads. The plan that allows for twenty days (that is, twenty-four hours of time spent logged in) is likely the best value for most researchers.

You should carefully choose your package since, for example, the lowest-level monthly passport will expire exactly thirty days after you book it. It also seems strange to American eyes that the site has no plan that allows for unlimited downloads, but Germans in general are a people more used to limits and less into the "all you can eat" concept. Taking screenshots of the pages is also not explicitly disallowed under Kirchenbuchportal's terms and conditions.

To purchase an Archion subscription, log in to Archion and click your username, then click Buchungen. Under Gebuchtes Paket, click Jetzt informieren. If you would like a one-month subscription, click Buchen under 1 Monat Privater Nutzer, and if you would like a one-year subscription, click Buchen under 1 Jahr Privater Nutzer. On the next page, fill in any information that is not already prefilled on the next page: Adresse (street address), PLZ (ZIP code), and Stadt (town and state, such as *Los Angeles, CA*). Click Weiter and choose whether to pay with PayPal or credit card. Follow the payment instructions. For the credit card option, you should check both check boxes on the next page, then click Kostenpflichtig bestellen. Then click Klicken Sie hier, um Ihre Bestellung sicher über PAYONE bezahlen. Fill out the standard credit card form. Once you've submitted your subscription information, you'll receive a confirmation e-mail that tells you when the subscription is active.

POWER-USER TIP

First Search FamilySearch.org
Some church records now digitized by Archion are available for free either in microfilm or online through FamilySearch.org. Since Archion is a paid subscription site, try the free FamilySearch.org first.

SEARCHING AND BROWSING THE CHURCH BOOKS

You can look at what church books are available (and call up digitized pages if you paid for a subscription) from either Suche (Search) or Browse. Suche allows you to enter a village name directly while Browse starts on the archive level, then drills down to the church districts, parishes, and finally individual volumes of the church books. In neither case are names in the registers searchable. In cases where the registers on Archion are also found on microfilms in the FamilySearch system, you'll need to make note of two things about the site. First, new technology has made many of the scans on Archion crisper than those on the microfilms. And second, Archion lists the holdings of a particular parish by what's in each *Band* (volume) whereas FamilySearch cataloging, especially on older microfilms, usually lumps together volumes and may obscure chronological gaps in the records. Here's a step-by-step guide for getting to the church registers each way.

STEP-BY-STEP EXAMPLE: SEARCHING FOR A VILLAGE NAME ON ARCHION

1 Click Suche on the main page. In order to get an idea what the archives have (even if the church book isn't digitized), check the Register box under the Quellen section on

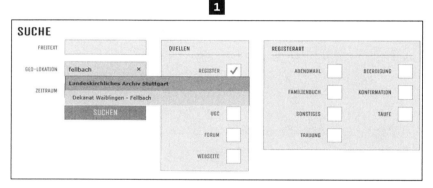

the Suche page. Type in the name of the village in the Geo-Lokation field. If a blue box pops up beneath the field, review the village name and click it if it matches what you're looking for.

2 Click Suchen. The search results are displayed. Click on the link for the time period for which you are looking to view the record.

STEP-BY-STEP EXAMPLE: BROWSING FOR RECORDS ON ARCHION

1 From the main page, click Browse, then drill down using each subsequent box to find the records you're looking for on the next page. Items in green are digitized and available to be viewed online.

2 When you would like to view records online, click Im Viewer anzeigen when you have a record selected.

1

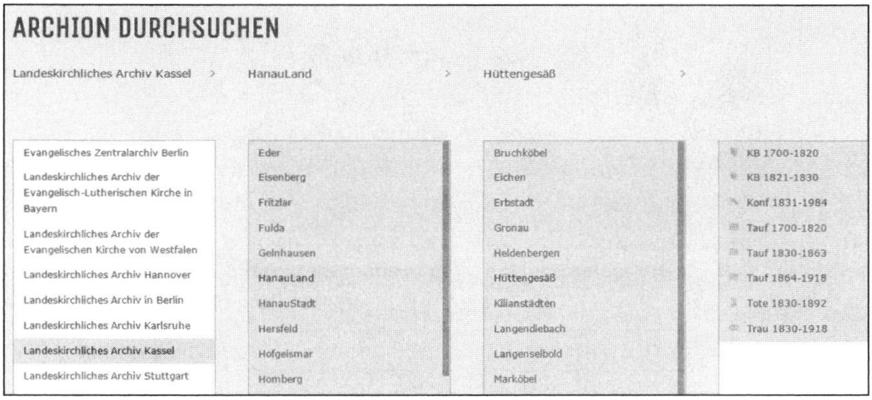

2

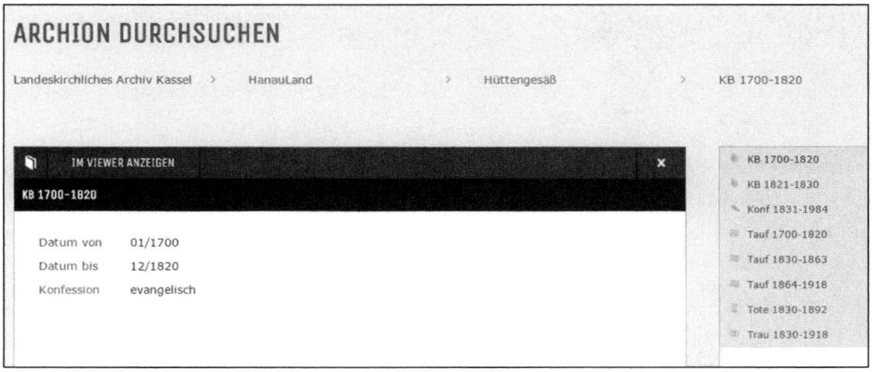

3 View the digitized microfilm. Use the frame along the left-hand side to navigate through the images. Use the tools on the top-left of an image to control zoom and rotation of the image, and click the printer icon button to download a file as a PDF.

TIPS, CAVEATS, AND FORECASTS

Archion is definitely a moving target. Digitization of the church registers is continuously happening, and the site expects to expand its digitization efforts in the English version. The pace of digitization varies from state church to state church, and Kirchenbuchportal is not committing to a specific completion date for the remaining 75 percent of church registers. The entity hopes that additional Protestant state churches will join the Archion effort and is open to working with the Roman Catholic churches in Germany, too. While waiting for the cooperative digitization effort, some of the individual archives may have individual projects not yet preserved on Archion. To learn more about these, check out a list of church archives and their Web contact information at **<www.archion.de/de/kontakt>**.

KEYS TO SUCCESS

▦ Determine what Protestant church registers Archion has digitized and which will be useful for your research.

▦ Know what the different levels of subscription will get you. Registering for an account is free and allows you to post on Archion's Forum. But if you think that Archion's records will be useful to you, you'll have to spring for a paid "passport" to look at actual pages of the church registers and download copies of them.

▦ Don't waste your money. As with other paid subscription sites, make sure that the resources you're looking for aren't already available for free on another website (or aren't available on a website you already pay for!).

PART THREE

ANSWERS TO YOUR RESEARCH QUESTIONS

9

HOW DO I IDENTIFY MY ANCESTORS' PLACE OF ORIGIN?

The late Arta F. Johnson, a linguistics professor who also wrote and lectured on German genealogy, had a knack for illustrating her presentations with some of the most showstopping anecdotes. One time, she was talking about how crucial language skills and historical background were to finding the German village of origin. Johnson said a woman had come up to her at a conference, somewhat breathless, and said that her ancestor's *Heimat* was written on his tombstone as *Großherzogtum, Baden*, showing her a photo of the tombstone as evidence. "But never in twenty years of searching have I been able to find the village of *Großherzogtum* on any map of Baden. Can you help me?" she asked. Johnson replied that indeed she could. "You see," Johnson recounted telling the woman, "there's no comma between the words, and *Großherzogtum* means 'grand duchy,' referring to the 'Grand duchy of Baden,' a political unit at the time." Johnson reported that the woman slinked sheepishly away.

The woman's confusion in Johnson's story is not unusual, and as you work your way into more specialized sites, you need to have your wits about you in determining what areas those sites are talking about. The upshot is that you need to challenge your assumptions about where you will find records from your ancestors' villages as well as how to work with the information you have available—a region of origin or a port of embarkation, for example. In this chapter, we'll discuss some strategies and resources you can use when taking this important step in your research.

CHANGES IN POLITICAL DIVISIONS

Throughout the book, we've been harping on Germany's history of decentralized records that goes along with its fractured political history. But this repetition is necessary for you to avoid the fate of many novice researchers who go into a search with blinders on and therefore may fail to see many of the records relating to their families.

In America, we're used to a linear formation of new political units—unsettled land became territories, those territories became states, the states were divided into counties, and the counties often were further divided into municipalities (like towns, townships, cities, and/or boroughs, depending on the particular state) as their populations grew.

But in the German states, the evolution of political units was rarely linear. For example, a duchy (ruled by a duke) could be divided into three parts so each son could have a share. Later, one son's dynastic line dies out, and his family divvies up his share amongst descendants of the other two lines. But then some towns in one part of the duchy are co-owned by a Catholic archbishop's state, and one of the co-owners buys out the other. During the early 1800s, a "mediatization" process granted church officials' holdings to the nearest secular state. Finally, during Prussia's ascent into German preeminence, the formerly independent state (along with its villages) became a province of the Prussian kingdom.

Why delve into this complexity? Because which noble jurisdiction owned a village during a particular time period will affect in which local, regional, state, and religious archives the village's records will be found today. Essentially, you need to always "think in triplicate"—to coin a German phrase, *denken dreimal*—when looking to place your immigrant's village in the context of the overall German map. You'll need to keep three key time periods in mind when plotting out when and where your ancestors lived:

- **Historical (before 1871):** Where was your ancestral town historically located? In most cases, this includes the time your ancestors immigrated (e.g., before 1871).

- **Second Reich (1871–1918):** How did your ancestors' hometown fit into the German Second Reich, when Germany first united as a nation-state? This time frame is especially helpful since the catalog at FamilySearch.org **<www.familysearch.org>** uses these jurisdictions, and most of modern Europe's boundaries were set by the end of World War I.

- **Today (1945–present):** How was your ancestors' hometown affected by post-WWII conventions and civil mergers? Where can you find it today?

Chapter 5 of *The Family Tree German Genealogy Guide* (Family Tree Books, 2013) contains a full listing of current and historical names of German government divisions. The local civil registration office known as a *Standesamt* houses the birth, marriage, and death records unless these records have been passed on to an archive. While this was mandated by a new German law several years ago, often these documents are still held at the village level back to the point they were initiated.

USING COMPILED VILLAGE HISTORY BOOKS

For a number of reasons, finding that your German ancestor's village has an *Ortssippenbuch* (a publication also sometimes called an *Ortsfamilienbuch*) is like finding a gold mine. These books are ordinarily compiled by an expert local historian or genealogist who has sorted together all the families found in a particular locality from the beginning of the community's records (the sixteenth or seventeenth centuries or, in some cases, as early as the fifteenth century) to either the present day or a relatively recent cutoff date.

Generally, these books are organized as follows: The surnames in the locality are alphabetized, and families with the same surname are listed chronologically by marriage date, along with birth, marriage, and death places and dates. This information, along with any other finds (e.g., occupation), comes from church books, civil registration records, and court, tax, and land documents. Some of the books even cross-reference families in other *Ortssippenbücher*.

Each family group in the book is given a number (starting with the first alphabetized family), and if any of the family's children's marriages are known, those children are given their own family numbers—you just have to go to that number to continue the line. Likewise, the father and mother in a family listing will include their fathers' family numbers so you can continue a line backward in time. The family listings make heavy use of abbreviations and symbols to give the maximum amount of information in the minimum amount of space; for example, preceding the dates of vital information: an asterisk (*) is

POWER-USER TIP

Distinguish Town Names
Remember that many German village names are used multiple times in the country. Read enough of the site to know that you have the right town named *Burg*!

used instead of "born"; a double *o* linked together means "marriage"; and a cross indicates "death." Most of these books were published in the decades after World War II, in some cases as a way of using the immense amount of data that the Nazi Party had required from people to prove their Aryan origins. As a result, their typeface is usually easy to read.

Please note that these books are secondary sources and the information you find in them should be verified with the original records wherever possible—even experts can make mistakes! Also, carefully examine the books' structure; some of the volumes contain multiple villages (all part of one church parish, for instance) and separate out the families by village in the volume. Other books were designed primarily for the village's local population and eliminated entries for people who were not represented by a current descendant in the village. The German areas in which the most of these books have been published are Rhineland-Palatinate, Hesse, Baden, Württemberg, Ostfriesland, Saarland, and Waldeck.

Volumes called *Dorfbücher* sometimes list lines of descent within families or houses, but concentrate more on the history of the village as a whole. Since the history of many German villages stretches back eight hundred to one thousand years, these *Dorfbücher* are often thick volumes, filled with abstracts of the early documents and photos of historic houses and people of the village. When such a *Dorfbuch* is published during a village's anniversary year, it is often called a *Festbuch*, but will contain the same type of material as a *Dorfbuch*.

You've already learned about the large database of the *Orts-* books and other similar types of records at Genealogy.net **<www.compgen.de>**. But several other sites have databases like the *Orts-* books that you can reference online. These include the following:

- Genealogie und Haus-Chroniken im Gebiet nordwestlich von München (Genealogy and House Chronicles in the area north-west of Munich) **<www.genealogie-kiening. de>**: Region northwest of Munich

- Militsch-Trachenberg in Niederschlesien **<www.militsch.de>**: Silesia (now in Poland)

- Familienbuch Euregio (Euroregion Family Book) **<www.familienbuch-euregio.eu/guest.html>**: Border triangle of Germany, the Netherlands, and Belgium
- Quellen zur Geschichte von Borgholz und benachbarter Orte (Sources for the History of Borgholz and Neighboring Cities) **<www.mynetcologne.de/~nc-kornhomi/borgholz2.html>**: Eastern Westphalia

GEOGRAPHY-SPECIFIC LISTS OF EMIGRANTS

Many times, you will not be able to find a document naming a village or city but instead find the name of a political jurisdiction. In this instance, hope that the political jurisdiction named is not *Prussia* (*Preußen*), since by the mid-1800s, Prussia ruled more than half of what became the Second German Empire in 1871. (All is not lost if this is the case—but you need to hope that you can narrow the origin down to a particular Prussian *Provinz* before conducting an effective search.) If you have the name of a specific German state or Prussian *Provinz*, you'll find in this section that many sites have lists of emigrants from that geographic area. Also remember that, as you saw in chapter 6, Genealogy.net may also have databases and indexes like these.

In this section, I'll identify some regional resources that can help you find your ancestors if you suspect they have come from a particular part of Germany. Since the exact village of origin is often among the pieces of information included in such emigrations lists, they can be the record that puts important data in your hands.

Auswanderung aus Südwestdeutschland
(Emigration from Southwestern Germany)

This site **<www.auswanderer-bw.de>**, operated by the Landesarchiv Baden-Württemberg (the Baden-Württemberg State Archives), has the records of more than 250,000 emigrants from Baden and Württemberg, most from the nineteenth century (image **A**). Most of the names come from emigration indexes kept at the various civil registration offices. In the left frame, click Suche nach Auswanderern, then the Standard link next to the binoculars to view the search form (image **B**). *Vorname* means first name and *Name* is for

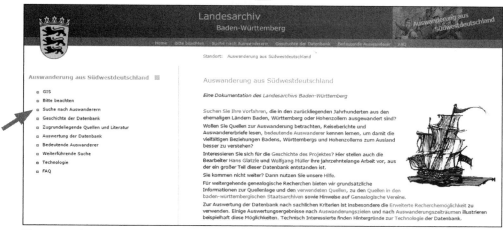

The state archives in Baden-Württemberg hosts a database of more than 250,000 emigrants.

The Landesarchiv Baden-Württemberg allows you to narrow your search by name, emigration year, or even emigration century.

the family name. To search for a place of origin, first click a letter under the Herkunfts-ort field. Once you click the letter, the drop-down box will fill with standardized village names from which you can choose. You can search for a specific emigration year in the Emigr.jahr field, or you can simply narrow by century by clicking one of the check boxes under that field (*Jh.* is an abbreviation for *Jahrhundert*, which means "century"). You can narrow by any combination of destination places using the Erdteil check boxes.

Finally, you can choose whether to do a standard or full text (*Volltext*) search in the Suchmodus field, the number of results per page in the Treffer pro Seite field, and the way you would like the search results sorted in the Sortierung field. Click Daten Suchen to search. When the search results display, you can click the magnifying glass for a record of interest to bring up detailed information about the emigrant, including important pieces of information such as year of birth, marital status, occupation, the number of adults and children emigrating along with the subject, and a brief description of the circumstances that led up to emigration.

Reinhard Hofer's Bavarian Emigrant Name Index

Reinhard Hofer is a German family history researcher, and he has compiled an index of more than seven thousand emigrants from Lower and Upper Bavaria, Upper Palatinate, and Frankonia in the years ranging from about 1830 to 1914 **<home.arcor.de/emigration-research>**. His sources include state and church archives and private collections, and the site lists just names and years. In order to get more detailed information about someone

Tracing Urban Ancestors

Think your ancestors lived in the big city? First, a point that will be review if you've read *The Family Tree German Genealogy Guide:* When you're told that an ancestor came from a large city in Germany, especially if the emigration was earlier than the second half of the 1800s, realize that this may really mean the person came from a small village close to that large city, just as someone in America may come say they're from "New York" when they really hail from East Meadow on Long Island.

But more and more emigrants *did* come from the burgeoning urban areas as the nineteenth century wore on, and city directories are great sources of information for these emigrants. Berlin's city directories from 1799 to 1943 are available at **<digital.zlb.de/viewer/cms/82>**. Ancestry.com, FamilySearch.org, and Genealogy.net all have some collections of city records and city directories, plus citizenship papers and tax rolls. Individual cities (especially larger ones) will also have their own archives. These resources can help you learn about your urban ancestors—and if they really lived in the city at all.

in the index, you will need to contact Reinhard through the contact links on the site. To browse the index by first letter of last name, click Emigrant name index along the left side of the page.

Bremer Passagierlisten (Bremen Passenger Lists)

This site <www.passagierlisten.de> has more than seven hundred thousand emigration records compiled from passenger lists housed at the Staatsarchiv Bremen (Bremen State Archives). Most of the records are from the early 1900s, but a few are from the 1800s. The passenger lists are similar to others of their kind; information contained in the records may include age, marital status, occupation, place of residence, nationality, and destination. Use the Familienname field on the left side of the page to search by a last name. The original passenger list may be viewed by clicking on Originale link while looking at a computerized record.

GermanImmigrants1850s.com

This site <www.germanimmigrants1850s.com> contains information about more than 450,000 Germans who arrived in the United States in the 1850s. The site was created by Crafted Knowledge, a Web development company that specializes in bringing public domain data to the public for free. The information in the database most likely comes from passenger lists, although this is not explicitly stated on the site. To search for an emigrant, first click a letter at the bottom of the page, then click a combination of first and second letter of the emigrant's last name and finally a surname (remember to look for as many spelling variations as you can think of). A list of the records in the database with that surname displays. Click a record to view information about the emigrant, including age, occupation, ship name, and destination.

Auswandererlisten des ehemaligen Herzogtums Braunschweig (Emigration Lists of the Former Duchy of Brunswick)

This site <www.thomas-erbe.de/ahnen/buch/001.htm> has an index of names found in a book written by Fritz Gruhne that contains emigration lists from 1846 to 1871 from the former Duchy of Brunswick, which was centered in the city of Brunswick. However, the index does not contain names from the city of Brunswick or the *Landkreis* of Holzminden. To view actual records, you would need to look at the book itself or order the microfilmed version from FamilySearch (film number 1045468 item 10). Records in the book will generally contain the name of the emigrant, the date of emigration, and the names of the emigrant's parents. Scroll down from the top of the page to view names in the index as well as from what page in the book they are taken.

List of Buer Emigrants to the USA

This site <www.buer-us.de/Book1a.html> contains emigration records from the village of Buer, which is about ten miles east of the city of Osnabrück. The site is arranged alphabetically by last name. Click a name to view detailed biographical information about each emigrant with that name. Sources for this information include Buer church records, emigration lists at the Lower Saxony State Archive, and passenger and immigration lists, as well as stateside records like censuses and church books. Keep in mind that many of these sources would be classified as secondary.

Regionale Auswandererdatenbank CLAUS (Regional Emigrant Database CLAUS)

This site <routes.de/tinc?key=aDbVINBZ&formname=CLAUS> contains almost six thousand records of emigrants from the modern-day *Landkreise* of Cloppenburg and Vechta, which are situated about thirty miles southwest of Bremen. The exact source of the information is not explicitly stated other than that it comes from the Oldenburg State Archives. However, based on the data they contain, they seem to be extracted from civil emigration lists. The records range from 1830 to 1875 and can be free-form searched using the text box at the top of the page next to Aktuelle Ansicht: Alle Einträge. Information contained in the records may include age, marital status, parents' names, occupation, place of birth, place of residence, nationality, and destination.

CUXAUS

This site <www.hapaghalle-cuxhaven.de/auswandererdatenbank> has about six thousand emigration records from the modern-day *Landkreis* of Cuxhaven, which is in the northern central part of Lower Saxony and includes the city of Cuxhaven. The records range from 1830 to 1930 and document mostly emigrants to North America. From the main site, click Akzeptiert, zur Datenbank to view the records in the database. According to its main page, the site is still in a test phase. Records may contain date of birth, place of birth, place of residence, parents' names, emigration year, and destination.

Oldenburger Jahrbuch (Oldenburg Yearbook)

This site <www.honkomp.de/damme-auswanderung> has around four thousand records from the former Amt Damme in the former Grand Duchy and later Free State of Oldenburg, which includes Damme, Holdorf, and Neuenkirchen in modern-day southwest Lower Saxony. Records generally only contain the year of emigration, place of residence, and other family members traveling with the emigrant and range from 1830 to 1880. Most of the emigrants were heading to North America. From the main page, click Contents overview, then on the next page click List by name of the emigrants. The best way to browse the records is probably by the letter group links at the bottom of the resulting page.

Emslanders to the American Mid-West

This site <www.emslanders.com> has more than thirty-five hundred entries of church and civil registration records from Emsland (modern-day western Lower Saxony along the border with Belgium), passenger lists and indexes, some stateside records from the Mid-west, and some secondary sources compiled by other researchers. Each entry has a lot of detailed information about an emigrant (to the point of being almost biographical), much of which is secondary. Many records are also accompanied with a source statement tying back to primary sources. From the main page, click one of the letters corresponding to the first letter of the emigrant's last name to get started.

German Genealogical Research Service Emigrants Database

This site <www.ggrs.com/emigrants>, operated by researcher Sabine Schleichert, has about nine thousand emigrant records from all over modern-day central Europe. The free PDF versions of the lists detail the year of emigration, the territory of residence, the destination, and any companions. For one hundred euros, Sabine will provide the exact place of origin for the emigrant as well as any other information about him or her contained within her database (including the source of the information). From the main page, click the relevant link under To the lists.

Emigration from Lippe to the USA

This site <www.lippe-auswanderer.de/htm/auswanderer-usa-eng.htm>, operated by the Naturwissenschaftlicher und Historischer Verein für das Land Lippe e.V. (Natural Science and History Association for the Lippe Country), has secondary biographical information for emigrants from the *Landkreis* Lippe in northeast North Rhine-Westphalia. Lippe includes the cities of Bad Salzuflen and Detmold as well as many other towns and villages. As its name implies, the site focuses on emigrants who left for the United States and contains information on thousands of emigrants. From the link above, click Data of emigrants, then select a first letter of last name and a last name to see the detailed data. Click the link for an emigrant to see more detailed information about that person.

Mecklenburg Emigrant Database

The Institute for Migration and Ancestral Research (IMAR) has partnered with the Immigrant Genealogical Society (IGS) to create this database that currently contains about twenty thousand emigrants <www.immigrantgensoc.org/searches/imed/igs-imed. html>. The site itself only has an index of surnames contained in the database. However, if you provide them with information like your ancestor's age, hometown, occupation, and year of emigration (plus a requested donation of ten US dollars), IGS volunteers can search the database for you ancestor and print seventeen fields worth of relevant information—plus instructions on how to order copies of original records—if they find a match. If they find multiple possible matches, they'll send a list of options for you to evaluate.

Auswanderung Neuhauser Bürger (Emigrants of Neuhausen ob Eck)

This site <www.lang-germany.de/Archiv/Auswanderer_/auswanderer_.htm>, maintained by Kurt Lang, contains a few hundred emigration records from the village of Neuhausen ob Eck in the former Württemberg. They include mainly 1800s records for residents heading to Poland, Russia, Switzerland, France, and the United States. The information comes from town records. Scroll down from the top of the page to see individual records. Information included in the records are destination, age, occupation, and family members also emigrating.

Das Auswander-Archiv Nordfriesland (The North Frisian Emigrant Archive)

The Nordfriisk Instituut, a Danish organization, runs this site <www.nordfriiskinstituut. de/indexausw_e.html>, which contains about five thousand emigrants from North Frisia, the northwestern part of the former Duchy of Schleswig that is now part of the German Land Schleswig-Holstein. The index cannot be browsed; it must be searched. Click databank-inquiry to search by family name, town, and date.

Auswandererliste Rheinenser (Rheine Emigrant List)

This list of several hundred records <www.rheineahnen.de/listdoc/auswand.htm>, mostly from the 1800s, was compiled by Wilfried Brümmer, a native of the list's subject city of Rheine (west of Osnabrück and north of Münster in North Rhine-Westphalia). Like many of the other databases, this one contains biographical information that has been compiled and is secondary in nature, so you'll need to verify it.

Auswanderung aus dem Rheingau (Emigration from Rheingau)

This site **<www.rheingau-genealogie.de/seite16.htm>**, maintained by Norbert Michel, contains around one thousand emigrants from the Rheingau region of Hesse, which is about twenty miles west of Frankfurt. The data contains the place of residence, destination, the date of emigration, and comments about the emigration (many times including occupation and companions). The sources of the information are generally secondary in nature. On the site's home page, click Auflistung der Rheingauer Auswanderer (PDF-Datei) to browse the records.

Emigration out of Schleswig-Holstein, 19th Century

This site **<www.rootdigger.de/Emi.htm>** is maintained by Klaus Struve, a researcher who lives in Kiel. The site contains almost one hundred thousand emigrants from Schleswig-Holstein in the 1800s. Click a letter along the left side of the page to download a Word file that contains the estimated or exact date of birth, destination, and details of the emigration (many of which are not actual emigration records but accusations by authorities that a person may have emigrated illegally).

Genealogical Research in Schleswig-Holstein

This site **<www.hans-peter-voss.de/gen/e>** is operated by Hans-Peter Voss, a researcher from Steenfeld, and contains a few emigrant list links, including Emigrants from Schleswig-Holstein to America, 1636–1667; Dithmarschen emigrants, 1868–1920 (about thirty-six hundred people); Rendsburg emigrants, 1868–1884 (more than five hundred people); and Emigrants from the island of Fehmarn, 1871–1882. Click the links from the home page to view the data. The site also has useful information about old German handwriting and historical maps of Prussia and the German Empire.

Amerikanetz

This site <www.amerikanetz.de/beitraege/?&no_cache=1&L=0> contains links to many smaller lists of emigrants from Westphalia in the 1800s. The best method to use the site may be to search by name or village using the text box at the top containing the word *Suchbegriff*.

KEYS TO SUCCESS

- Begin your research by finding your ancestor's name and town of origin—the Web has plenty of resources, including digitized town histories and lists of immigrants.

- Use *denken dreimal* as your mantra: "Think in triplicate" about which political units your ancestor's village belonged to: historical, Second Reich, modern.

HEIMAT TIC-TAC-TOE WORKSHEET

Sometimes searching for your ancestors can seem like a cruel game stacked against you. But with careful research, dutiful documentation, and proper consideration of the time periods involved, you can track down your ancestor's *Heimat*. You can download a Word-document version of this worksheet at <**ftu.familytreemagazine.com/trace-your-german-roots-online**>.

Name of village: _____

Alternate spellings: _____

_____

	Historical (pre-1871)	Second Reich (1871–1918)	Modern (1945–present)
Political jurisdiction (Noble entity/district)			
Church parish (Catholic/Protestant)			
Standesamt (Civil registration)			

10

WHERE ELSE CAN I ACCESS CHURCH RECORDS?

You've already seen that some of the megasites (principally Ancestry.com **<www. ancestry.com>**, FamilySearch.org **<www.familysearch.org>**, and Archion **<archion.de>**) are the marquee sites for church records of our German-speaking ancestors, but you don't have to stop there. These records—which the late John T. Humphrey called "the heart and soul of German genealogy"—can be found on an increasing number of websites. A number of these include records from German-speaking areas outside of today's Germany, but I've included them here because many Americans have ancestors from these areas. Note that more religious archives—those that run their own websites—will be covered in chapter 12.

All of the following sites are written in German or French, so you will put your new-found translation skills from sites noted in chapter 3 to good use. Beware the English versions of each site; content may have been stripped out to avoid having to initially translate and constantly maintain multiple language versions of the site. View the site in its native language and attempt to use Google Translate **<translate.google.com>** or another translation service to keep much as of the original website as possible.

KIRCHENBUCH VIRTUELL

Bürgernetz Bayreuth e.V (Bayreuth Citizens' Network Association) is a nonprofit organization in the Bavarian city of Bayreuth that supports a wide range of projects. One of those projects happens to be Kirchenbuch Virtuell (Virtual Church Book), which is an effort to digitize church books from towns and villages surrounding Bayreuth as well as the city itself **<www.kirchenbuch-virtuell.de>**. This site contains church records from the late 1500s through the 1900s from areas surrounding Bayreuth in northern Bayern (Bavaria). To see which villages are available before spending any money, click Aktuelles und Wichtiges from the navigation menu on the left side of the page, and scroll down.

To access the site, click Benutzerkonto erstellen (Create a user account) from the main page (image **A**), then fill out the user registration form. When you're finished, go

A

The Kirchenbuch Virtuell site houses more than three hundred years of church records from northern Bavaria.

Erklären Sie bitte mit nachstehendem Formular Ihren Beitritt zum Verein.
Laden Sie das entsprechende Formular auf Ihren PC und füllen Sie es mit Ihren Daten aus.
Drucken sie die erforderlichen Formulare aus und senden Sie sie vollständig ausgefüllt an den Verein.

☐ **Anmeldeformular 14/12/2007,19:05 74.64 Kb**

☐ **Informationen zu unserem Bankkonto 14/12/2007,19:15 18.34 Kb**

☐ **Formular zur Auswahl der Bücher / Gemeinden 14/12/2007,19:17 46.62 Kb**

Sie können uns unter **info@kirchenbuch-virtuell.de**

eine E-Mail senden. Wir freuen uns über jeden konstruktiven Beitrag!

In order to use Kirchenbuch Virtuell, you'll need to print out and submit forms found on the site.

back to the main page and click on the three links at the bottom of the page one at a time, and print out each page (image **B**). Fill out the two registration forms (one is for membership in the church book club and one is to indicate which church books you would like to access). Mail the completed forms to the address listed at the bottom of the instructions page. Wire the amount required (forty-two euros, plus ten euros for each parish) to the account listed on the information page. Once the organization has received your completed registration forms as well as the required fees, you will receive a password that you can use to access the church books you would like to see.

MATRICULA

Matricula is a free pilot project by an Austrian nonprofit organization called ICARUS that seeks to digitize, as its name implies (*matricula* is Latin for "register"), the vital records kept by the Catholic Church in the region. The project **<www.icar-us.eu/cooperation/ online-portals/matricula>** has placed more than seven million pages of church books online so far, including Catholic records from the 1500s to the 1900s from the following diocese archives: St. Pölten, Oberösterreich (Upper Austria), and Wien (Vienna), covering the modern states of Upper Austria, Lower Austria, and Vienna in northern Austria; Passau (southeastern Bavaria near the border with Upper Austria) in Germany; and Breslau (now Wrocław; southwestern Poland near the border with the Czech Republic) in Poland.

From the URL above, click Zum Archiv (To the Archive) to access the site's records (image **C**). The directory along the left side is organized first by country, then by diocese archive, first letter of the village, and finally village. When you find the village you're looking for, click the + symbol next to its name. The details about that village will appear to the right. Click the link for Liste der Bände der Gemeinde (List of volumes of the parish) to view the village's collection (image **D**). Click the church book you are interested in.

C

Matricula contains digitized Catholic records from churches in Austria, Germany, and even Poland.

D

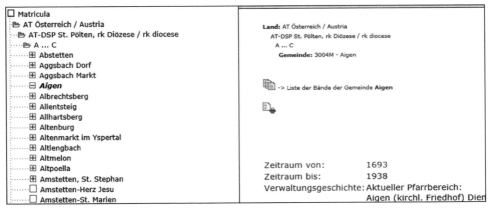

Matricula's records are organized by country, then by diocese, first letter of the village name, and village name. Each village's page displays what records are available for that village.

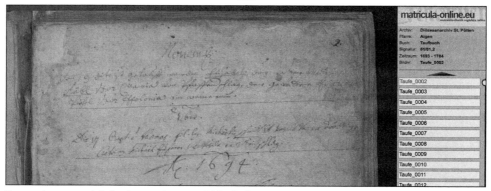

You can browse certain books page by page at Matricula.

The detail for the church book displays. Click zum Buch (To the Book) to view the church book if you see a camera icon (image **E**). The first image displays in a new window. Use the controls (most of them intuitive) along the bottom of the screen to go from page to page and zoom in and out.

STAATSARCHIV FREIBURG

The free Staatsarchiv Freiburg (Freiburg State Archive) **<https://www2.landesarchiv-bw.de/ofs21/olf/struktur.php?bestand=10028>** has digitized its holdings of church book duplicates that served as civil registration records in the Grand Duchy of Baden from 1810 through 1875. Freiburg is the archive for the southern part of the former Baden, and therefore its holdings concentrate on that area, reaching as far as Bühl to the north and the Swiss border to the south. In addition, the collection has Catholic, *Evangelisch* (Evangelical), and Jewish church and synagogue book duplicates from 1810 to 1875 in towns in the southern part of the former Grand Duchy of Baden (from Bühl in the north to the Swiss border in the south and from the French border in the west as far as Bonndorf in the east).

From the URL above, click Strukturansicht mit Suche a village name along the left side of the page. The list of available books from that village appears to the right. Click the Archivalieneinheit einsehen (Look at archive entry) link for the book you would like to view. Note that only twenty entries are displayed on each page, and most villages have multiple pages. Instead of having to page through, you can click Alle next to the page navigation buttons to display all entries for that village on one page (image **F**). It may be easiest to click Bild 1 (Image 1), then move through the book page by page using the intuitive navigation controls along the top of the page. To make things even easier, many of the

The state archive in Freiburg has digitized its church book duplicates, sorted by village.

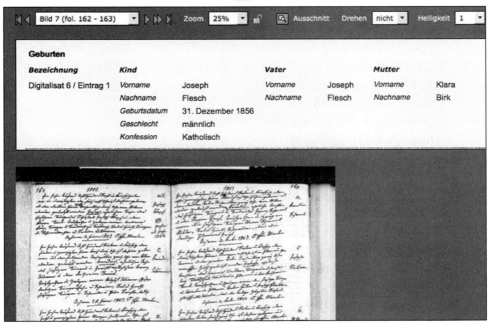

Many of the books available at the Staatsarchiv Freiburg have been indexed by FamilySearch, and these indexes appear next to the book's scanned pages for reference.

pages have been indexed by FamilySearch, and the indexed material appears above the image so that you don't have to read the pastor's handwriting (image **G**).

ARCHIVES DÉPARTMENTALES DU BAS-RHIN

At varying times over the last 150 years, Alsace was under the control of both the French (between the world wars) and the Germans (under the Second German Empire and during Hitler's regime). France introduced civil registration in 1792, and the practice continued even when the area came under German control in the 1870s (which was around the time that civil registration was begun in most of the rest of the Second German Empire). Many of the town names in this region are German in etymology and have German-speaking people living there. The northern half of Alsace is now known as Bas-Rhin (Lower Rhine), and the archive there has done an excellent job of digitizing not only its civil registration holdings but its Catholic and Protestant church books as well <etat-civil.bas-rhin.fr/adeloch/index.php>. This free archive has Catholic and Protestant church records (1600s through late 1700s) as well as civil registration (1792 through early 1900s) records from Bas-Rhin.

From the site's home page, click the check box labeled J'accepte ces conditions to accept the site's terms and conditions (you should translate and read this), then click Accéder à la version graphique. When the screen pops up, start typing the name of the village you're looking for, and you should quickly see the selection area narrowing down possible villages with those letters at the beginning. Click the village name that you are interested in (image **H**). Find the point in time you're looking for along the timeline at the bottom, then locate the correct book that contains the time frame you are interested in.

Note that if you see a translucent purple outline above the books, you are looking at church records; at the beginning of each purple outline, the system tells you what denomination and parish the group of books is for. If you don't see a translucent purple outline at the top, you are looking at civil registration records. Click the book you want to look at twice. The record book is displayed. Navigate through the pages using the arrows and slider at the bottom, and control zoom and brightness using the buttons at the top right.

ARCHIVES DÉPARTMENTALES DU HAUT-RHIN

Like Du Bas-Rhin, the southern half of Alsace called Haut-Rhin (Upper Rhine) bounced back and forth between French and German control: French until the Second German Empire and between the world wars, and German during the Second German Empire and World War II. These free archives <www.archives.cg68.fr> contain civil registration records (1792 through early 1900s) from Haut-Rhin, which has been part of France since World War II but has a significant German population.

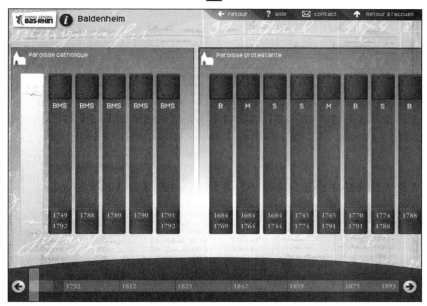

The archives of the Bas-Rhin has digitized civil and church records for the towns in its historical jurisdiction (such as Badenheim) and organized them by time period and type.

I

In the Haut-Rhin archives, you can search for a variety of records, including decade census tables (*tables décennales*), birth records (*naissances*), marriage records (*mariages*), death records (*décès*), publications of marriages (*publication de marriage*), and lists of Jews (*register des noms des juifs*).

From the URL above, click the Services tab. Along the left navigation pane, click Actes d'état civil. On the search form (image **I**), select the village you're looking for in the Commune field. If you know the specific type of record you are looking for (indexes, births, marriages, deaths, etc.), you can select it in the Type d'acte field. And if you have a specific year you are looking for, you can enter it in the Recherche par année field. In the dropdown, you can select Egale à (Exactly), Inférieure à (Before), Supérieure à (After), or Entre (Between). Click the Rechercher button. The available civil registration books appear below the search form. Click the magnifying glass on the right for the book you want to look at. The civil registration book is displayed (image **J**). Use the arrows along the top of the image viewer to scroll from one page to the next, or select a specific image using the ller directement à la page dropdown.

WITTGENSTEINER FAMILIENDATEI (WITTGENSTEIN FAMILY FILE)

This website <www.wittgensteiner.net> is run by Jochen Karl Mehldau, and he uses it to manage requests for information from his Wittgenstein Family File that he himself has composed over the course of the last thirty-three years. His database (image **K**) is a derivative source that lists the primary source that the information was taken from. Mehldau used mainly Catholic and *Evangelisch* church books to compose the database but also consulted some books for information. Wittgenstein, the focus of the records, is in the southeastern part of the modern-day state of Nordrhein-Westfalen (North Rhine-Westphalia). The site has Catholic and *Evangelisch* church records in the area of Wittgenstein from as far back as the early 1500s in some villages and as recently as the late 1800s in some villages. Note this resource isn't free; the site charges fifty cents euro for each person located in the database and one euro per person for detailed information

POWER-USER TIP

Consult with Local Experts
Other local historians and genealogists may have done for their areas what Jochen Karl Mehldau has done for Wittgenstein. Use the information in chapter 11 to help you find village contacts to query.

You can browse available civil registration books on the Haut-Rhin archives' website.

While it focuses on a particular family's genealogy, the Wittgenstein Family File includes transcribed marriage records that will be helpful for nonfamily members as well.

Die Griese Gegend in Mecklenburg

Online seit Januar 2006
Last Update: 09.07. 2015

Familienbräuche in Mecklenburg

Willkommen auf meiner Homepage zur Griesen Gegend (GG). Alle meine Mecklenburger Vorfahren stammen aus dieser Region.

Doch WAS und WO ist das?

Ich möchte Sie auf meiner genealogischen Homepage etwas über die Griese Gegend informieren, gleichzeitig aber auch viele Informationen über Personen und Ereignisse der Griesen Gegend, sowie Hinweise für die Ahnenforschung, bieten.
(Wenn Sie meine Seiten längere Zeit nicht besucht haben, klicken Sie bitte im Menü auf „*aktualisieren*"!)
Die wichtigsten Seiten habe ich mit einem ! gekennzeichnet. Für "Neulinge" der GG sind alle Seiten interessant!

Viel Spaß!

Informationen	Daten	Sonstiges
Wo und Was ist die Griese Gegend? (*incl. Karten*) !	Kopulationsregister, Trauregister (1800-1875) !	Niedergeschriebenes *über die* Gr. Gegend
Liste der Ortschaften der Griesen Gegend !	Kopulationsregister, Trauregister (1876-) !	Norddeutscher Leuchtturm (Zeitschrift)

While only covering the Griese area of Mecklenburg, Die Griese Gegend contains useful marriage registers for villages in the region.

Rekonstruktion vernichteter und verschollener Kirchenbücher

Die wahrscheinlich einzige Möglichkeit, verschollene oder vernichtete Kirchenbücher zu rekonstruieren, besteht wohl darin, alle weltweit in Form von Geburts-, Tauf-, Heirats- und Sterbeurkunden, Kirchenbuchabschriften, Stammbäumen, Familienstammbüchern, Ahnenpässen und ähnlichen Dokumenten oder auch in der Literatur vorhandene Daten zu sammeln. Ich habe begonnen, dies für die Kreise Arnswalde und Friedeberg zu tun, da hier kaum noch Kirchenbücher vorhanden sind, oder sie in den vielen Metern ungesichteter Akten in deutschen und polnischen Archiven verstauben und in naher Zukunft nicht zugänglich sein werden. Es ist bekannt, daß oftmals mehrere Gemeinden in einem Kirchenbuch geführt wurden. Dies habe ich zunächst außer Acht gelassen. Als Ort ist zunächst immer der Geburtsort gemeint. Später ist es durchaus möglich, die Daten einzelnen Kirchenspielen zuzuordnen.

Ich hoffe, daß jeder, der auf diese Seite stößt, die ihm vorliegenden Dokumente durchsieht, und mir die Informationen zukommen läßt. Es sollte sich dabei um einigermaßen zuverlässige Daten handeln, also keine spekulativen. Ich werde mich bemühen, die Liste möglichst kurzfristig nach Eingang neuer Informationen zu aktualisieren. Das Format der Daten ist ohne Bedeutung, da die Listen manuell erstellt werden, auch wenn dies unter Umständen einen erheblichen Arbeitsaufwand darstellen kann.
An dieser Stelle ein herzliches Dankeschön denen, die bereits an der Datensammlung mitgewirkt haben.

Es sind zur Zeit nur Seiten angelegt, für die mir schon Daten übermittelt wurden. Wer also Daten von noch nicht aufgeführten Orten hat, sollte mir diese unbedingt schicken.

Kreis Arnswalde

Althütte
Altklücken
Arnswalde
Bernsee
Bergmühle (Wohnplatz zu Nantikow)
Berkenbrügge mit Althorst
Bußberg mit: Grüneberg, Räumde, Rohrfort, Zietenfier
Friedenau
Fürstenau
Göhren
Granow
Hagelfelde
Hertelsaue mit: Buchthal Forsthaus, Buchthaler Mühle, Idashain, Lüdertswalde, Luisenau
Hitzdorf

The home page for the Gschweng family has some transcribed church records from villages in the historic Arnswalde and Freideberg regions, now in Poland.

(such as godparents or place of residence). Contact Mehldau at *jkmehldau@arcor.de* for more information.

DIE GRIESE GEGEND IN MECKLENBURG

This free website **<griesegegend-online.de>** is dedicated to the Griese area of Mecklenburg, which corresponds to the southwestern part of the modern-day German state of Mecklenburg-Vorpommern, roughly centered on Ludwigslust. Transcribed marriage registers are available from many villages in this area, and you have access to transcribed baptismal records if you happen to have ancestors from the village of Kirch Jesar. For the marriage records, click the Kopulationsregister, Trauregister links for the year range you're researching (image **L**). For the Kirch Jesar birth records, click Taufregister Kirch Jesar.

HOMEPAGE DER FAMILIE GSCHWENG AUS GREIFSWALD

This free site **<www.gschweng.de>** is dedicated to the history of the Gschweng family, but it also has some transcribed church records from the surroundings of Arnswalde (now Choszczno, Poland) and Friedeberg (now Strzelce Krajeńskie, Poland). Along the left frame of the page, scroll down to the Neumark section, then click Kirchenbücher. In the right frame, click the village you are interested in to see what records have been transcribed for that locale (image **M**).

KEYS TO SUCCESS

- After you've checked the megasites that have oodles of German church records, look for smaller sites that have targeted areas.

- Scope out what you can get for free. Most websites are free for users, but some require you to purchase use of the records.

- Don't overlook websites hosted by private individuals or families, as these will sometimes have church records from a wider area.

- Remember that if you have not found a German hometown for your ancestor, sites covering areas outside of today's Germany are worth a look if you suspect your ancestor came from there.

11

HOW DO I CONTACT PEOPLE AND PLACES IN GERMANY?

No cybercafé can compare to physically going in person to a German *Biergarten* or other outdoor eatery. But a menu of websites and strategies can help you hit the ground running when that trip to an ancestor's *Heimat* becomes reality. Whether your specific desire is to track down modern-day relatives, find a German researcher, or complete some virtual task in Germany, this chapter will put some items in your toolbox that will prepare you well for such an adventure.

While many German institutions lagged a bit behind their American counterparts in moving to digital systems, e-mail is now available when querying about most things. While this may not apply to small or out-of-the-way villages (and less widespread in the area of the former East Germany), you can usually find some avenue of electronic communication to the area you're seeking.

You also need to leave behind those American presuppositions we talked about in chapter 2—remember Germany's relative compact geography as well as its penchant for locally kept records. Note that to get the best results from contacting German archives, you'll need to follow some special procedures. These will be covered in chapter 12.

CONTACTING A VILLAGE OF ORIGIN

Many individual villages in Germany now have their own websites, and finding them can be as easy as plugging in *www.* plus the town name and the default German web URL suffix of *.de* or by putting the village name and the name of the German *Land* it lies in into a Google search. If either of these ways bears fruit, write your request—about town records, archives, or just the fact that you plan to visit—in English unless you are relatively fluent in German. They will usually reply in German, so you'll need to translate that reply using tools discussed in chapters 2 and 3.

Of course, you need to realize that the person who receives your e-mail at (or for) the German village may not have even a passing interest in genealogy, and it's helpful to recognize that by making your initial e-mail short—and, perhaps, by merely asking for the recipient to direct you to someone who is interested like a local historian, a *Heimatmuseum* (a history museum in the town devoted just to that village), or a civil or religious archive for records of village.

If the e-mail given on the town website doesn't yield a reply or you couldn't find a website for the town, then it's time to play the "tourist dollars" card. Germans are nothing if not savvy businesspeople, and if you write to the area's tourist board, it often will forward your message to an official of the village for an answer.

CONTACTING POTENTIAL RELATIVES

We've talked about looking for surname concentrations in chapter 3, but what if you have a lead on a particular individual or city? Well, here's something that's certifiably better than in America—all of Germany's landline telephone numbers (and some cell numbers, too, if the individuals opt in for this) can be found together in one online directory—*Das Telefonbuch* <www.dastelefonbuch.de>. This directory is also a more comprehensive search than American phone books (and their online equivalents) because Germans can't just tell the phone company they want their numbers unpublished. Rather, they need to furnish a narrowly drawn security reason for this to be done. As with America, however, the trend among young people is to have only a cell phone.

> **POWER-USER TIP**
>
> **Lead with Zeros**
> Be aware that when dialing telephone numbers in Germany, you may omit the first zero from city codes (like our area codes) inside Germany when using a landline. However, you'll need to include the leading zero if you are dialing from outside Germany.

You can find most German businesses and individuals in *Das Telefonbuch,* an online repository of addresses and phone numbers that German citizens with landline telephones have to opt out of to be excluded from.

The logistics of using this national telephone directory are fairly straightforward. The home page (image **A**) displays boxes marked Was (literally, "what"—which is where you put the surname of the person or business name being searched) and Wo ("where," if you want to limit your search to a certain town).

Click on Finden to execute a search. Other types of searches can be done using the icons in the middle portion of the page (the lower portion of the home page is not shown on the image, as it contains advertisements, as does the rotating "billboard" right under the Was/Wo/Finden boxes). Among the other specialized searches that can be done by clicking on the icons in the middle are ones that add social networking contact information; a reverse search to use if you have a phone number and want the individual's name; and directories by business categories (like the old yellow pages). Remember you can get a rough translation of the names of the special categories by feeding the page through Google Translate **<translate.google.com>**.

STEP-BY-STEP EXAMPLE: SEARCHING DASTELEFONBUCH.DE

1 Call up the home page. Fill in a name—surname first, then a given name in the Was box and a city in the Wo box (both are optional). For this example, we used the surname *Schneider* and the city *Kaiserslautern*.

2 View the results of the default search, which include both business and personal listings. To limit the search for just individuals (which also will bring back a few mom-and-pop business listings, too), click on Personen.

1

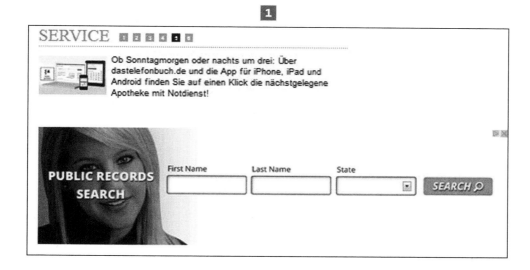

2

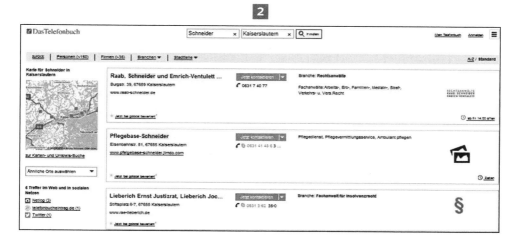

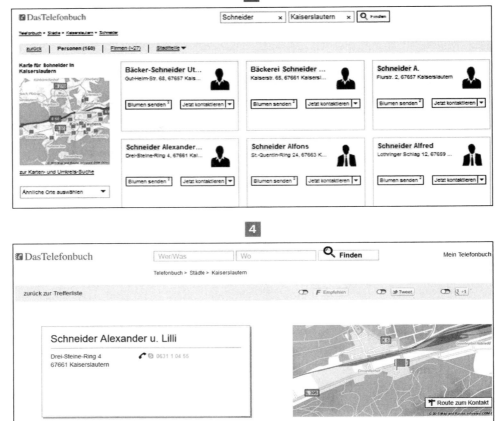

3 Filter your search by clicking Personen. The Personen search will also bring back a few mom-and-pop business listings, and in this case shows 150 individuals. Select a result (here: *Alexander*) by clicking on that name.

4 View full information on the individual: his marital status (married to Lilli), his address and phone number, and even a map locating his home.

CONTACTING A GERMAN PROFESSIONAL

This is a case in which America and Germany have something in common: both have organizations for their professional genealogists. However, just as genealogical periodicals written in English are indexed in PERSI (the PERiodical Source Index), while

German-language publications are found in Der Schlüssel (literally, "the key"), so too are English and German professional researchers organized into separate groups. The Association of Professional Genealogists (APG), based in the United States, has some German members. However, a much smaller organization of German-speaking professional researchers is called the Verband deutschsprachiger Berufsgenealogen (which the group translates as the "Association of German-speaking Professional Genealogists").

The Germany-based group's website can be accessed in German, English, or French. Like the APG, the German organization has a code of standards that each member must

Reisen to Riesling

I had searched for many years—including about a dozen trips to the Family History Library in Salt Lake City—to find the German hometown of my surname immigrant ancestor, Johannes Beÿdeler. Finally in 2010, just a half an hour before I would have left Salt Lake City again empty handed, I found his 1727 marriage in the records of Gerolsheim, a village in the German *Land* Rheinland-Pfalz. As luck would have it, I'd already booked a trip to Europe, primarily to see the once-in-a-decade Passion Play in Oberammergau. Gerolsheim would fit nicely into the itinerary immediately upon my arrival in Germany.

As I continued to make plans for the trip, I read a short article on Wikipedia **<www.wikipedia.org>** about the village and found a town website; however, the website listed no e-mail to contact anyone there! According to the Wikipedia article, Gerolsheim was part of a collective municipality (in German, *Verbandsgemeinde*) called *Grünstadt-Land*, and the Gerolsheim website showed that the village was connected with other wine-producing villages in a tourist consortium called *Leiningerland*.

The Leiningerland website listed an e-mail, so I sent a short note asking if someone could meet me in the village and allow me to purchase any collectibles—steins, stained-glass crests, history books—from Gerolsheim. In just a few days, I was contacted, in somewhat passable English, by the town's deputy mayor, Klaus May. He wrote that he would be glad to meet me at his home and then take me to see the *Ortsbürgermeister* (village mayor) named Erich Weyer.

And so it went. My girlfriend and I drove from the airport in Frankfurt to Gerolsheim, where May and his wife met us. We walked with May to the town hall where Weyer was waiting. I purchased the Gerolsheim collectibles, and the mayor cracked open a bottle of the locally produced Riesling wine. Our trip was well under way! We toured through the town and later the Mays and another couple took us to Germany's largest wine festival in Bad Dürkheim—all on our first day!

Today, I'm friends with Klaus May on Facebook **<www.facebook.com>**, and we occasionally exchange messages. Truly, the tourist bureau created a great connection for me with my ancestral hometown!

adhere to, though the German association's list of standards are stereotypically German in that they are lengthy and specific. Also like the APG, members of the German association are not specifically credentialed as genealogists (two American-based groups, the Board of Certification for Genealogists and the International Commission for the Accreditation of Professional Genealogists offer, respectively, "Certified Genealogist" and "Accredited Genealogist" designations).

The decision to hire a professional, especially one in a different country, can be difficult and perplexing. First of all, you may be one of those researchers who takes pride in doing his own work. And, of course, some people just plain think that everything in genealogy (maybe in life, too) should be free. If a hobbyist does not see the value in paying a professional—someone with specialized experience who will get a pedigree correct, probably in a fraction of the time—nothing the professional will do will be adequate.

But if you do see the potential value of hiring a pro, you need to address personal and logistical concerns. Feel free to ask for several references in America who you can contact about the professional's work. Give the professional a complete rundown on what sources you've consulted and what you either know or suspect about the ancestor being researched. In exchange, the pro should be able to give you a short summary of what his or her plan is for your research money.

And speaking of money, you'll need to know how to pay the foreign genealogist. This will vary from one professional to another. Some have American bank accounts that allow them to easily deposit American checks, and more are taking credit cards. PayPal is a popular option, too. If you run into a situation in which the only option is a transfer to a German bank account, you can do that, also—and we'll go over how to do so as part of chapter 12's section on paying for German archives.

KEYS TO SUCCESS

- Research what resources are available for your ancestor's hometown. Making contact with a German village can be as easy as entering the name as a URL or by Googling it. In addition, *Das Telefonbuch*, a national telephone directory for Germany, has a variety of search features and can help in your research.

- Check with tourist bureaus if there's no village website or you get no response from the locale's listed contact.

- Be realistic about your foreign-language writing skills: Good English beats bad German in communicating by e-mail or letter.

- Check references and ask for a research plan before hiring a professional genealogist in Germany.

12

WHAT ORGANIZATIONS AND ARCHIVES CAN HELP MY RESEARCH?

I admit that just a few years ago, I finally had a need for German archival holdings (in this case, older vital records from one of the Berlin civil registration offices). And I'll further admit that I approached the task of ordering the records for a professional client with a bit of trepidation—not knowing how the Germans would respond, if at all (I feared that they were like their American bureaucratic counterparts).

So I somewhat tentatively e-mailed my request and received a response the next day saying that I could indeed make my request by e-mail, but that I needed to know the correct one of the many civil registration offices in Berlin. Fortunately, I had successfully determined this from some of the same online tools listed in this book. I didn't receive a response, so I waited a few days before e-mailing again. As it so happened, photocopies of the vital records had already been mailed, along with an invoice requesting a deposit in the archive's bank account. I had underestimated German efficiency—and the German registrar's trust that payment would be remitted! I also realized that I better find out how to get the payment made in the form they requested (which is the subject of the Paying the Bill in Germany sidebar).

We've looked at some of the repositories in previous chapters, mostly concerning their partnerships with major online outfits such as FamilySearch.org **<www.familysearch.org>** and Ancestry.com **<www.ancestry.com>**, but many more organizations and repositories also have holdings available online or a noteworthy Web presence. While you may not yet be able to receive the instant gratification of finding digitized records on these sites from the comfort of your home office, the ability to communicate electronically with local society and repository experts will help point you in the best direction to focus your research. Some of these organizations can be found in the Vereine portal on Genealogy.net **<wiki-de. genealogy.net/Portal:Vereine>**, profiled in chapter 6.

SOCIETIES AND ORGANIZATIONS

Genealogical research is not done in a vacuum. One of the biggest themes in the industry over the past few years has been collaboration, in particular online collaboration. While you'll have to avoid many pitfalls (e.g., blind faith in the information found across the Internet), many reputable societies and organizations have online (and offline) resources available that can help you in your German ancestry research, and these groups create invaluable networks of researchers. This portion of the chapter will focus on some of the most helpful and prominent organizations, first in America, then in Europe.

In America

With so many Americans having German-speaking ancestry, German-focused genealogical organizations across the country are available to help you. Some are specialists in Germans from particular geographic areas while others cater more generally to German genealogists. Some of these organizations have well-developed websites with helpful databases, while others have a lot of FAQ-type information online. But all of the groups listed in the following sections have Internet contact points for you to consider as springboards, and the members of these groups may be able to answer some of your questions.

AMERICAN HISTORICAL SOCIETY OF GERMANS FROM RUSSIA (AHSGR)

According to the group's mission statement **<www.ahsgr.org/index.htm>**, the AHSGR is "an international organization dedicated to the discovery, collection, preservation, and dissemination of information related to the history, cultural heritage, and genealogy of German settlers in the Russian Empire and their descendants." Membership entitles one to reduced rates on research in the society's records and document translation services as well as reduced prices on many of the media available from the society. When you join, you will also be listed in the society's surname/place directory, which you can search for like-minded researchers.

THE GERMAN SOCIETY OF PENNSYLVANIA (GSP)

Located in Philadelphia, the GSP **<www.germansociety.org>** was founded in 1764 to protect German immigrants from exploitation as they traveled to the American colonies as well as after they arrived. Today, the society dedicates its efforts to preserving German heritage, going so far as to offer scholarships for undergraduate students majoring in German language and literature. Members subscribe to the society's quarterly newsletter, borrow items at their library (which holds seventy thousand volumes), and receive discounts to some events.

GERMANIC GENEALOGY SOCIETY (GGS)

Based in St. Paul, Minnesota, the GGS **<www.ggsmn.org>** has a library holding twenty-two hundred books and periodicals. The society publishes a quarterly journal and has a surname database to help researchers get up to speed with where others have gotten so far on a specific family. An annual membership is relatively inexpensive, coming in at fifteen US dollars as of the time of writing.

MID-ATLANTIC GERMANIC SOCIETY (MAGS)

MAGS **<www.magsgen.com/index.php>** strives to facilitate research on Germanic genealogy in the mid-Atlantic region. The group has a library inside the Shenandoah County Library in Edinburg, Virginia, and members receive a quarterly newsletter as well as free consultations with professional genealogists. Annual memberships are very affordable.

PALATINES TO AMERICA (PALAM)

PalAm **<www.palam.org>** promotes the study of Germanic immigration to North America. They hold an annual conference and have seven regional chapters across the country (in Colorado, Illinois, Indiana, New York, North Carolina, Ohio, and Pennsylvania). The Palatines sponsor a quarterly scholarly journal and provide fee-based research and translation services. In addition, a name index to the *Palatine Immigrant* journal has been published four times per year since the United States bicentennial in 1976.

SACRAMENTO GERMAN GENEALOGY SOCIETY (SGGS)

The SGGS **<www.sggs.us>** publishes the acclaimed quarterly journal *Der Blumenbaum* and provides research assistance to those seeking German ancestors. The society also hosts monthly meetings that feature informational lectures from leading professional researchers in the field.

OTHER GROUPS

While not as widespread or well-known, many other groups in the United States have resources that you might find useful. Many of these focus on particular states or regions. Pennsylvania actually has two of these notable regional resources. The Pennsylvania

German Cultural Heritage Center <sites.google.com/site/pagermanchc/home>, right in the middle of Pennsylvania German country at Kutztown University, hosts annual events and preserves historic artifacts designed to showcase Pennsylvania German culture and history. The Pennsylvania German Society (PGS) <www.pgs.org/default.asp> has a similar mission. The PGS publishes a journal several times per year and hosts an annual meeting. Farther west, the German Interest Group—Wisconsin <www.gig-wi.com> has a surname database and a periodic newsletter for a nominal fee, while the German-Texan Heritage Society (GTHS) <www.germantexans.org> down south promotes the preservation of German cultural heritage in Texas, hosts an annual conference, and puts out a quarterly journal.

Two other resources focus on more specific groups of immigrants. Not to be confused with the American Historical Society of Germans from Russia, the Germans from Russia Heritage Society (GRHS) <www.grhs.org/index.html> is dedicated to bringing together people interested in discovering the unique history of Germanic Russians, with a library in North Dakota and a quarterly magazine. Even more of a niche group, the Society of the Descendants of the Schwenkfeldian Exiles <www.schwenkfelderexilesociety.org> is dedicated to the 209 people who followed the Schwenkfelder Church in Silesia and decided to head to the New World when facing religious persecution in the 1730s.

In Germany

As was noted earlier in the chapter, many genealogy groups based in Germany have websites that "hook onto" the Genealogy.net web portal. Some, however, don't have that connection but *do* still have information helpful to researchers for particular areas of Germany. These resources can be especially helpful to you once you've placed your ancestors in the old country.

In addition to the resources listed in this section, the site Many Roads <www.many-roads.com/2014/12/14/german-genealogical-societies>, while focusing on the Rabideau-Hensse family history, boasts a helpful list of German genealogical societies, many of which specialize in a particular region of Germany. Browse through it if you've already located your ancestor's village of origin.

ARBEITSGEMEINSCHAFT FÜR MITTELDEUTSCHE FAMILIENFORSCHUNG E.V. (THE CENTRAL GERMAN FAMILY RESEARCH ASSOCIATION, OR AMF)

As its name suggests, the AMF <www.amf-verein.de> is dedicated to family history research in Central Germany, as well as Berlin, Brandenburg, Mecklenburg-Vorpommern, Saxony, Saxony-Anhalt, and Thuringia. The group maintains an archive in Leipzig and also has an online store that sells electronic books (most—if not all—of the books are written in German). The group's website features a link to a database where you can search to see for members researching the same family name/place combination. Members also receive a quarterly magazine.

DIE MAUS—GESELLSCHAFT FÜR FAMILIENFORSCHUNG E. V., BREMEN
(THE MAUS—THE FAMILY RESEARCH SOCIETY, BREMEN)

This group has an extensive online database <www.die-maus-bremen.de/index.php> that includes civil registration records from around Bremen, more than thirty thousand citizenship applications spanning from the 1600s through 1900, some very old tax lists, and wills covering 1599 through 1899 (just to name a few of the site's resources). The MAUS publishes a semiannual newsletter and consults with members about research problems they are facing.

REPOSITORIES AND CIVIL ARCHIVES

If you have the chance to visit a German archive, some of the most prominent of which are described below, remember a couple of important guidelines. First, you should always endeavor to make an appointment, as the records you need could be stored offsite and have to be ordered ahead of time. In addition, professional researchers at the archive could be limited in time. Second, you should not expect the employees at the archive or repository will have the time or any desire to help you read and interpret the records you may find, so come prepared with historical context and whatever documents you may need to help you interpret records (such as a German script and Fraktur reference).

Another important note is that archived civil registration records for births, marriages, and deaths could quite possibly be held at the local *Standesamt*. In order to access these records, you will need to get in touch with the local registrar, and as outlined in chapter 9, German federal law dictates "blackout" time periods before records are freely available: 110 years for births, 80 years for marriages, and 30 years for deaths. Some of the local offices as well as the larger archives will be willing to see if a record exists before requiring payment, then they will bill the requester along with a copy of the record. To find the correct civil registration office, start by finding the village in *Meyers Gazetteer of the German Empire* on Ancestry.com <search.ancestry.com/search/db.aspx?dbid=1074>. In write-ups about each village, *Meyers* will indicate whether the village had its own office or, if not, to which other town's office it was attached. Then you can browse the listings held by modern-day *Lande*, keeping in mind that your ancestors' records may be in small city archives or in an archive with statewide holdings.

In this section, I'll outline some resources you can use to find civil registrations and other records kept by the government.

Archivportal

Archivportal is a highly useful service of the German Digital Library, especially if you're struggling to find your ancestors in other archives' records. The site **<www.archivportal-d. de>** serves as a front to the complex archival structure in Germany. The database is organized by place, so the first step (as always) will be locating a village of origin for the ancestor in question. Next, you should gather basic genealogical data about that person using church or civil registration records before you attempt to consult these types of archives (though, in certain cases, the church and civil registration records may be held in these archives). That said, once you have the basic information about someone, the information in the regional and local archives can help you learn more granular information about the lives of your forebears. You can search for a place directly, but keep in mind that information from one village or town could certainly be kept in an archive in a neighboring place.

The best way to go about finding an archive of interest is probably to just browse its listings by modern-day German *Land*.

1

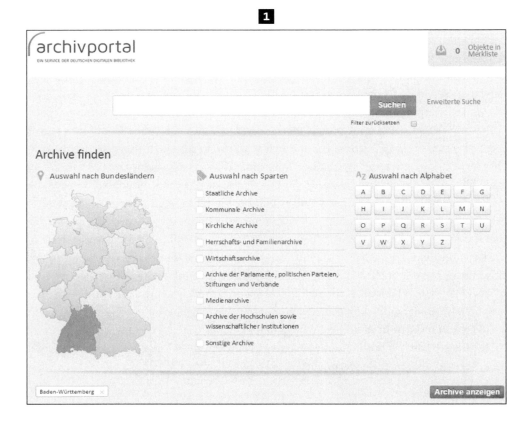

STEP-BY-STEP EXAMPLE: SEARCHING FOR RESOURCES ON ARCHIVPORTAL

1 From the main page, select the current *Land* that encompasses the area you're researching (Baden-Württemberg in this case). Then click Archive anzeigen.

2 Browse through the results on the Archive tab for any towns or cities that are near your area of interest.

3 If you see an archive you're interested in, click its name. Then you can either click Objekte anzeigen to view Archivportal's listing of the archive's holding or Homepage to go directly to the archive's website for more information about the repository and its holdings.

2

ARCHIVE	OBJEKTE	

Bundesland ▾	Sparte ▾	Anfangsbuchstabe ▾

Baden-Württemberg ×

▶ Archiv des Deutschen Caritasverbandes e.V.

▶ Archiv des Main-Tauber-Kreises

▶ Archiv soziale Bewegungen in Baden e.V.

▶ Archivum Rhenanum - Digitale Archive am Oberrhein / Archives numérisées du Rhin supérieur

3

▶ Eberhard-Karls-Universität Tübingen, Universitätsarchiv

▶ Evangelische Landeskirche in Baden. Evangelischer Oberkirchenrat, Landeskirchliches Archiv

▼ **Landeskirchliches Archiv Stuttgart**

Landeskirchliches Archiv Stuttgart, Balinger Straße 33/1, 70567 Stuttgart

👁 **Objekte anzeigen**   🔗 Homepage   ℹ Infoseite

   ▶ Evangelische Landeskirche in Württemberg. Landeskirchliches Archiv
   ▶ Landeskirchliches Archiv Stuttgart (Archivtektonik)

▶ Gemeindearchiv Assamstadt

Prominent Archives with Digital Holdings

Some of the many archives in Germany have particularly good digital assets, and some are worth noting separately because their holdings are essential for research (whether digital or not). They range from Germany's federal archive (unfortunately, not nearly the equivalent of America's National Archives and Records Administration) to a couple of digital libraries focusing on documents from the western German states of Hessen and Rheinland-Pfalz. Here, I'll outline some of these valuable digitized resources.

DAS BUNDESARCHIV (THE GERMAN FEDERAL ARCHIVE)

The German Federal Archive **<www.bundesarchiv.de/index.html.de>** does not centrally store civil registration records from across the country; those records are kept at the *Standesamt* level. However, the Federal Archive can be very useful in the context of military record research. Another large record set is the *Ahnenpass* collection, which were the multigenerational ancestor charts required to be filed by potential Nazi Party members to prove Aryan descent.

As morose as this context is, the information contained in them can be useful. In order to see if the records you seek are digitized, visit Invenio **<invenio.bundesarchiv.de/basys2-invenio/login.xhtml>**, which is the archive's online catalog. After registering, you will be able to search and browse the archive's holdings. Please note that all records in the archive were microfilmed and are available for viewing at the National Archives and Records Administration in College Park, Maryland, so if the records you seek are not digitized, contacting the stateside archives would be a more efficient route than attempting to access the records in Berlin.

DEUTSCHE ZENTRALSTELLE FÜR GENEALOGIE (GERMAN GENEALOGICAL CENTRAL OFFICE)

The holdings at this repository **<www.archiv.sachsen.de/6319.htm>** are mainly focused on the German state of Saxony, but they also hold material applicable to the wider German-speaking realm. The holdings have a vast scope, as they're organized by the German equivalent of a US state. But for people who live too far from the archive to visit, the staff will respond to written requests for lookups that take less than an hour. In order to determine if the archive holds something of interest to you, you can search its holdings using the Suche in Archivbeständen link. Many of the archive's church book holdings have been microfilmed by the Church of Jesus Christ of Latter-day Saints, so look there first for the village you seek.

HERDER-INSTITUT

If you have German-speaking ancestors from eastern central Europe in countries like Poland, Estonia, Latvia, Lithuania, the Czech Republic, or Slovakia, this archive

German Archives at a Glance

Building from chapter 9's *Heimat* Tic Tac Toe, in which you identified the jurisdictions under which your ancestor's village lay at various times, check out this list of potential types of archives you may encounter (and should seek out) when investigating your ancestors:

- **ADELSARCHIV:** archives of a noble family, which may include the equivalent of public records from when that family ruled an area
- **BUNDESARCHIV:** "national" archives of the Federal Republic of Germany
- **EVANGELISCH:** Protestant church archives, usually organized by the state churches
- **HEIMATMUSEUM:** technically not an archive, but may house archival materials from a particular village
- **KATHOLISCH:** Catholic church archives, usually organized by dioceses or archdioceses
- **KREISARCHIV:** archives of a district
- **LANDESARCHIV:** archives for a German Land (equivalent of a US state)
- **STAATARCHIV** or **HAUPTSTADTARCHIV:** "state archives" or "high state archives," though state in this context means an independent political unit of the old Holy Roman Empire
- **STADTARCHIV:** archives of a city (but usually includes the surrounding area)

is for you. Its holdings **<www.herder-institut.de/en/home.html>** are vast and include records like church books that were microfilmed during World War II. Some records have also been digitized; you can search the catalog at **<www.herder-institut.de/dshi/Bestaendeuebersicht/index.htm>** by clicking Suche.

HESSIAN REGIONAL HISTORY INFORMATION SYSTEM (LAGIS)

This site **<lagis.online.uni-marburg.de/en>** has a fully functioning English menu, plus atlases, maps, photographs, and gazetteers to help researchers gain a better understanding of what daily life was like in Hessen.

INSTITUT FÜR PFÄLZISCHE GESCHICHTE UND VOLKSKUNDE (INSTITUTE FOR PALATINE HISTORY AND FOLKLIFE STUDIES)

This repository **<www.pfalzgeschichte.de>** boasts a three-hundred-thousand-sheet emigration file containing about one million individual records, perhaps its most valuable genealogical resource. The Institute also has forty thousand books on regional history of the Palatinate, newspapers, and photographs. Many of the records aren't available online, so you'll need to contact the archive (see the Kontakt link along the right side of the page).

If you're able to locate your ancestor or his village of origin in the digital holdings of this repository **<www.dilibri.de>**, you may be able to paint some colorful details about your family's historical life in the Palatinate. One of the highlights of this website is its fully functional English version. Holdings include books, illustrations, maps, and newspapers.

CHURCH ARCHIVES

You've already learned about the large site Archion **<www.archion.de>** (in chapter 8) for records from many of the German Protestant state churches as well as efforts such as Matricula **<www.icar-us.eu/cooperation/online-portals/matricula>** (in chapter 10) that are digitizing some Roman Catholic records. And megasites such as Ancestry.com have created access to many church records of German ethnics in America. But finding out Roman Catholic records (and even some Protestant resources) in other areas requires using a smattering of smaller, church-run sites. This section gives a rundown of the websites of such church archives.

Roman Catholic

The Roman Catholic Church is somewhat prominent in the western part of Germany (along its borders with France, Luxembourg, and Belgium) and in the southern part of Germany (along its borders with Switzerland and Austria). If you have ancestors from these areas, they were possibly Catholic. Be sure to scrutinize stateside records as much as possible to try to determine if your immigrant ancestor and his family were Catholic or Protestant before doing too much focused research on one denomination or the other in Germany.

If you find that your German ancestor was indeed Catholic, you can search the German Catholic Church's website to see a map of the ecclesiastical borders **<www.katholisch. de/kirche/Deutschland>**. Click on the map to see each clerical district's headquarters address, e-mail address, and website, plus the name of the bishop in charge. Each one of these parishes has its own organization and archive, and you may find that some parishes are more helpful or organized than others. Also keep in mind that the records for the ecclesiastical province of Passau along the border with Austria are contained in the online repository Matricula **<www.data.matricula.info/php/main.php>**, profiled in chapter 10.

Protestant *(Evangelisch)*

Many of the parishes of the Evangelisch Church in Germany are participating in the Archion project, detailed in chapter 8. However, the following archives are not currently participating in Archion:

Paying the Bill in Germany

While you won't have any perfect options when it comes to making payments to German individuals or archives, completing complex international money transfers is definitely a case of "where there's a will, there's a way." Part of the reason for this is that, per insight from Europe-based professional genealogist Glen W. Covert, the Single Euro Payments Area or SEPA (which includes Germany and Austria) works opposite of how most Americans do business. In the United States, a person owed debt sends his address to the debtor, then the debtor responds with a payment that can be deposited. Within the SEPA, however, the person who is owed money provides the debtor with his bank account information rather than his address. The debtor then directly transfers the money from his account to the account of the person to whom he owes money.

Credit cards are likely your best option, as credit card companies generally guarantee transactions against fraud. However, not all American credit cards will automatically work internationally (some require a fee to do so), plus German archives generally will not accept credit cards. This leaves to sort through other money transfer services, such as:

- XOOM **<www.xoom.com>**: XOOM uses your (American) credit card to make a deposit directly into an archive's bank account. Obviously, you'll need the archive's banking information to complete this; the archives will provide this to you if this is its preferred method of payment. The base transaction fee is $9.99, so you want to combine bills whenever possible (for example, if you're going to have continuing needs from a particular archive, see if you can pay monthly rather than in several separate transactions that would each cost $9.99).

- TransferWise **<www.transferwise.com>**: TransferWise charges a much lower transaction fee (starting at three US dollars) but quotes currency conversion at what it calls a "mid-market rate." This rate will generally result in a more unfavorable conversion for you as compared to XOOM, neutralizing some of the fee savings. TransferWise, however, offers a 5 percent savings for those not needing immediate transfers.

- PayPal **<www.paypal.com>**: One of the most popular online payment options, PayPal can only transfer funds between two individuals or organizations that have PayPal accounts. While it helps further protect your credit card information, PayPal is not currently able to deposit money directly into a German bank account. As a result, you'll likely use it most when paying professional researchers who also have a PayPal account and prefer to be paid in this way.

- Bremische Evangelische Kirche **<www.kirche-bremen.de/index2.php>**: This *Gemeinde* covers the areas immediately surrounding Bremen. The Staatsarchiv Bremen **<www. staatsarchiv-bremen.de>** holds most of the church books from before 1920.

- Evangelisch-Lutherische Kirche in Oldenburg **<www.kirche-oldenburg.de/?1>**: Although it has no digitized holdings, this archive does at least list its microfiche holdings at **<www.kirche-oldenburg.de/themen/bildung/archiv/familienforschung/ microfiches.html>**.

- Evangelisch-Lutherische Landeskirche in Braunschweig **<www.landeskirche-braunschweig.de/aktuell.html?no_cache=1>**: This parish covers the areas immediately surrounding Brunswick (*Braunschweig*). None of its holdings have been digitized, so check to see if the Church of Jesus Christ of Latter-day Saints has microfilmed the records of the town you're interested in.

- Evangelischen Kirche in Mitteldeutschland **<archive.ekmd-online.de/portal>**: This branch of the Evangelisch Church, covering much of central Germany, is less centralized as far as records administration is concerned. Many of the parishes still hold their own records, while some regional archives have been established. Cross your fingers that the Church of Jesus Christ of Latter-day Saints microfilmed the records you're looking for; otherwise, you may need to try to get in contact with an individual church.

- Evangelisches Zentralarchiv in Berlin (The Evangelisch Central Archives in Berlin) **<www.ezab.de>**: Although this archive participates in Archion, it also holds many other documents tied to the administration of the Evangelisch Church since its creation in 1817 by Prussian authorities.

- Lippische Landeskirche **<www.lippische-landeskirche.de/1-4-36>**: This subdivision covers roughly the modern-day *Kreis* of Lippe in Nordrhein-Westfalen and does not have any digitized holdings.

Other Christian Denominations

As has been noted in part 2's chapters on major websites, many of the records from Protestant denominations most frequently used by German ethnics in America have been digitized by one of the major websites, such as those preserved by Ancestry.com's deals with the Evangelical Lutheran Archives as well as the many church records in the collection of the Historical Society of Pennsylvania. Notably, the Moravian Church's two archives have not gone the collaboration route, and we'll cover these resources in this section. In the case of many other denominations, whatever archives system they have is still off the online grid.

The Moravian Church Northern Province's archive **<www.moravianchurcharchives. org>** has records from congregations in California, Indiana, Maryland, Michigan, Minnesota, New Jersey, New York, Pennsylvania, and Wisconsin. If you have determined that your ancestor was a member of a Moravian congregation, this would be the place to look for possible records. If you are not able to visit the archive yourself just east of Allentown in Bethlehem, Pennsylvania, you can request research. You can fill out the online research request form, and the archive will get in touch with you with a cost estimate.

If you have Moravian ancestors that are from the southern half of the American colonies, this archive could be helpful. The website **<www.moravianarchives.org>** states that its researchers field a few complex genealogical inquiries per week, so sending them a detailed request shouldn't be a problem, and the lack of a language barrier is always a relief.

KEYS TO SUCCESS

▓ Comb through the holdings of German-focused archives and organizations, both stateside and in Germany.

▓ Look beyond the church and civil record offerings of big websites like FamilySearch.org and Ancestry.com. Many churches and regional archives have their own collections of records that either haven't been digitized or haven't found their way onto larger sites.

▓ Carefully consider the different methods of payment, and select the one that best reflects your needs and security preferences.

13

HOW CAN SOCIAL MEDIA SITES HELP?

Social media websites are a powerful presence on the Internet. Even if you normally only use Facebook as an electronic photo album, you may become a media maven yourself when you see some groups or pages that offer a bucketful of genealogy help! In addition, you may want to "put yourself out there" on social media sites as a way of attracting attention to your genealogy brick walls and interests. Co-host of the Genealogy Guys Podcast, Drew Smith, wrote *Social Networking for Genealogists* (Genealogical Publishing Company) back in 2009, and its insights on using social platforms like Facebook <**www.facebook.com**> for genealogy are still relevant.

In this chapter, we'll provide some ideas on using social media sites to your best advantage. We'll look at social media megasite Facebook first since it has the most utility for researchers.

FACEBOOK

Facebook's complex "page" and "group" structure gives it the most potential among the major social media sites to help in your quest to find German roots.

Groups

People with similar interests can create and administer groups, producing a forum that can help generate new research ideas as well as help with the toughest of research problems. With more than a billion registered users, you'll find a Facebook group for pretty much any topic, and German genealogy certainly hasn't been left out. Check out these family history-focused Facebook groups to see what they might be able to do for you.

GERMAN GENEALOGY

This group describes itself as a forum for "networking with those conducting German genealogical research, in order to provide help and resources to others researching German genealogy." Image **A** shows the setup of the group's page at **<www.facebook.com/groups/GermanGenealogy>**.

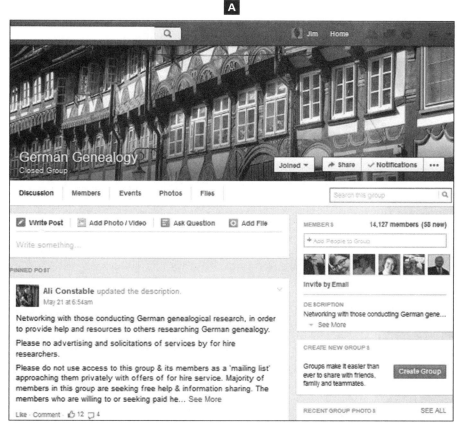

The German Genealogy group on Facebook is the largest and arguably most important forum available to German researchers on social networking sites.

The group's administrators aggressively fight spamming and attempts by anyone to solicit business, and the result is a reliable forum for thoughtful and helpful discussion. With more than fourteen thousand members as of this writing, someone in the group is bound to have run into a similar difficult issue that you're facing as you attempt to trace your German lineage. This group can also be used as a forum to request transcription and translation help for documents written in German.

According to the group's page, you should follow this step-by-step guide to receive assistance from other group members:

1. Post your image with a translation request.
2. See which members offer help.
3. Contact those members privately and ask if they can assist you further. Give basic details of how much you need translated, etc.
4. When you find someone who agrees, send images straight to them (either by e-mail or Facebook message, whichever they prefer), one at a time.

You may be able to find someone using this method who enjoys working with German documents and may be willing to transcribe and/or translate your document for free or at a fraction of the cost of contracting with a professional in the field.

One caveat to this group is that it is closed, meaning that you have to request membership, then wait for an administrator to approve it. As a result, it may take some time to get going depending on the administrators' response time.

Facebook serves up what it considers the "top posts" as part of your Facebook notification feed ("News Feed"); realize that what the algorithm considers "top posts" may not jive with your particular interests. Once you're accepted, you'll likely need to go to the group's page itself to see all postings and users' comments.

AHNENFORSCHUNG

Ahnenforschung means genealogy (or, literally, "ancestry research") in German, and likewise this group **<www.facebook.com/groups/358990344127948>** is naturally geared towards German genealogy, although it doesn't say so explicitly. With posts and administration in both German and English and close to four thousand members, this group can be a potentially valuable resource for sparking new ideas and gaining a better understanding of German genealogy. Again, this is a closed group, so you will need to wait to be approved by an administrator before you can post.

FEEFHS

FEEFHS stands for the Foundation for East European Family History Studies (what an acronym!). Although this group <www.facebook.com/groups/278430439787> doesn't necessarily bill itself as a research help forum (rather, the group's president would like to "direct the energies of the organization toward indexing and other record discovery projects"), plenty of posts ask for assistance and garner professional-level responses, like one detailing the difference between a *Kirche* (church) and a *Bethaus* (prayer hall).

At just about a thousand members, this group has considerably less breadth of membership compared to the German Genealogy and Ahnenforschung groups. However, FEEFHS offers a public group, meaning you don't have to wait for an administrator to approve your membership before you jump in and start posting. Try to be specific about the problem you are encountering or the piece of information you are trying to obtain. Note that this probably would not be a good forum for posting transcription or translation requests.

OTHER GROUPS

Facebook is a huge site, so you'll certainly encounter even more groups that you'll find helpful in your research. For example, a closed group called Genealogy Translations <www.facebook.com/groups/genealogytranslation> focuses on translations (from any language) in a genealogical context, as its name implies. You'll find many family-specific groups on Facebook as well. The site has a powerful search engine, so try searching *[family name] Family* in the box at the top of the page. People in these groups won't always be from the same lines of the family name, but you may be able to gain insight into what specific areas clusters of people with the surname you are researching came from or live today.

POWER-USER TIP

Consult with Multiple Users
The skill level of people on social media sites will vary and people may not clearly self-identify. You may want to collect a "second opinion" from a member of a different group before trusting information presented on these platforms.

Pages

Facebook has "pages" for pretty much anything you can think of (including articles on Wikipedia, which serve as topics that link to groups and pages, and user-created pages designed to promote a specific thing). Consider "liking" (i.e., following) the Genealogy field of study (search *Genealogy* from the Facebook main page), and you may soon find that Facebook's algorithms are tailoring your news feed to posts that have to do with family history research.

When you see interesting posts about genealogy, be sure to like the page that generated it, and over time you will notice that your news feed increasingly features the topic of genealogy.

OTHER SOCIAL MEDIA

Facebook is not the only social media tool out there. You can also get some leads and instruction by utilizing other resources as well.

Twitter

Twitter **<www.twitter.com>** is for what's known as microblogging, or sending messages ("tweets") that are limited to 140 characters. Further, tweets are organized, not by type or subject, but by hashtags, which are meant to categorize tweets and tie them to other messages sent across the platform. These are manually input by users sending the tweet by using the pound sign (#) to accompany messages. Needless to say, this does not create great conditions for in-depth discussions about genealogical research problems. However, while tweets must be short, they may contain clickable references to other websites or articles about German genealogy that may be helpful to you.

Like Facebook, Twitter has a news feed where you're able to view the tweets of accounts you "follow" in real time, and that's where Twitter's true utility lies. Try searching the name of the organization or town using Twitter's search feature along the top of the page, then click the Follow button. Genealogical organizations like Ancestry.com (@*ancestry*, image

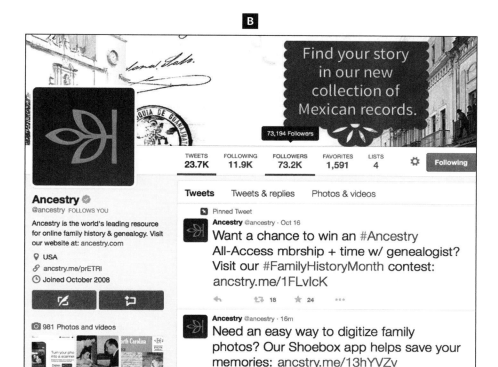

Many genealogical services and societies, such as Ancestry.com, share resources via Twitter. Ancestry.com sends its tweeted messages (which can view under the Tweets tab) to its seventy-three thousand followers.

B), publications like *Family Tree Magazine* (*@FamilyTreeMag*), and individual personalities in the genealogical community have Twitter accounts. You may want to follow German-themed organizations (for example, archives or genealogical societies) or German towns that you come across to stay on top of the latest happenings, as many of them have Twitter handles (another word for "accounts," indicated by the "at sign," @).

YouTube

Searching *German genealogy* on YouTube **<www.youtube.com>** yields quite a few videos specifically about the topic (image **C**). As with any information obtained from social media, try to verify the credentials and skills of the person posting the video before investing too much time watching instructional videos. Ancestry.com **<www.ancestry.com>** has a channel on YouTube **<www.youtube.com/user/AncestryCom>**; many of Ancestry.com's are available through their website as well.

YouTube users have uploaded thousands of videos related to German genealogy, from interviews with professional genealogists to Ancestry.com tutorials.

Other Resources

Other social media sites that generate some of the highest levels of traffic on the Internet are LinkedIn **<www.linkedin.com>** (professional networking), Pinterest **<www.pinterest.com>** (online pinboard), and Instagram **<www.instagram.com>** (photo and video sharing). While you may be able to find an interesting post here and there on the topic of German genealogy on these sites, your time likely will be better spent researching and discussing elsewhere.

KEYS TO SUCCESS

■ Engage with other researchers on social media sites to help you overcome research challenges and maybe even meet some family members.

■ Consider requesting membership to some of the German genealogy groups on Facebook, as these can be good forums for getting translations or help from other researchers. Be sure you're posting in the appropriate group before asking for assistance.

■ Like Facebook pages and follow Twitter users who share German genealogy content or can connect you to genealogy-related websites and articles.

■ Verify anything you find on social media, as users likely don't have to present their credentials or sources when posting information.

14

WHAT ELSE SHOULD I ADD TO MY TOOLBOX?

G iven the ubiquity of German-speaking ancestry, virtually any website with genealogical material can have some effect on German family history to some extent.
This book has attempted to give a complete rundown of the resources available
online that will benefit virtually every genealogist searching for German ancestors. Some
topics did not merit complete chapters (or didn't fit in the categories we've discussed so
far), so I'll cover them in this section.

Remember that genealogy is about more than just collecting names and dates. In order
to be exposed to more biographical information about your ancestors, you'll want to consult alternate resources to church and civil registration records. This chapter will dive
into some of the best of those resources that are available on the Internet.

GERMAN-LANGUAGE NEWSPAPERS AND PERIODICALS

Prior to World War I, German-language newspapers were the most prominent foreign-
language newspapers in the United States. Some of the top sources for German-language
newspapers in the United States are detailed below, along with links to places where you
can access newspapers from Germany. Get out your Fraktur reference, because if you

are able to find your ancestors in contemporary newspapers, you will undoubtedly learn more about their daily personal and public lives, which can serve to color all of the dates, places, and names that you have uncovered.

GenealogyBank

GenealogyBank **<www.genealogybank.com>**, a service of NewsBank dedicated to genealogy research, has many German-language newspapers from Philadelphia as well as the Pennsylvania German areas like Berks and Lancaster counties, along with scattered holdings from other states like Ohio and Illinois, just to name a few. There are also troves of English-language newspapers from German areas in the colonial era.

Chronicling America

Chronicling America **<chroniclingamerica.loc.gov>** is a service of the US Library of Congress, featuring many digitized images of newspapers spanning from the colonial area to around World War I. Many of these images are of German-language text and come from loci of German immigrant settlements. One other highly useful service on the website is the catalog of newspapers from across the country; the database is an amazing reference even if the title you're looking for is not available online. On each newspaper's entry, there is a link to known holdings of that title at places like state, local, and university libraries as well as at other types of archives.

German-North American Resources Partnership via WESS

This project's website **<www.wessweb.info/index.php/German-Language_Newspaper_Access_in_North_America>** serves as a directory for German-language newspaper holdings at various archives across the world. Most of the holdings are not available for online viewing, but if you see a small computer icon with a green arrow over top of it next to the name of the newspaper, you're in luck: You'll be able to view digital images of that title online. Some of the online holdings this website links to are contained at the following:

- Bavarica **<bavarica.digitale-sammlungen.de>**: A service of the Bayerische Staatsbibliothek (Bavarian State Library), Bavarica includes many digitized titles from Bayern (Bavaria) as well as an electorate that had historically been in union with Bavaria, Pfalz (also known as the Palatinate).

- Freiburger Historische Bestände—Digital **<az.ub.uni-freiburg.de/show/fz.cgi?pKuerzel=FZ>**: Freiburg University holds a large online collection of the *Freiburger Zeitung* (spanning 1784 to 1943 with missing years and issues) as well as other digitized newspaper holdings.

- ZEFYS **<zefys.staatsbibliothek-berlin.de>**: ZEFYS is an online service of the Staatsbibliothek zu Berlin (Berlin State Library). Its digitized holdings include newspapers from across the former Kingdom of Prussia, focusing on the area around Berlin but containing such oddities as the *Ägyptische Nachrichten* (*Egyptian News*) and the *Argentinisches Wochenblatt* (*Argentinian Weekly Paper*).

Allgemeine Auswanderungs-Zeitung (General Emigration Newspaper)

When emigration from Germany was at a high point in the mid-1800s, publisher Günther Fröbel sporadically published a newspaper geared towards people who were thinking about or planning on emigrating from Germany, as well as towards people whose relatives had recently emigrated. The newspaper printed passenger lists that are important for genealogy research, and you can view individual issues online spanning from 1846 to 1870 online **<zs.thulb.uni-jena.de/receive/jportal_jpjournal_00000025>**.

LINEAGE AND BIOGRAPHICAL BOOKS AND DATABASES

The sources detailed below would be considered secondary sources, so remember to find the primary sources from which they were compiled. Even so, they can be incredibly useful in pointing you in the right direction for finding those original records. They are all databases of names and places or digitized versions of original print materials now made searchable.

Die Ahnenstammkartei des Deutschen Volkes (The Pedigree Card File of the German People)

Originally begun in 1923 with positive collaborative intentions, this card file came to be used by the Nazi regime to prove or disprove someone's Aryan descent, which excluded Jewish, African, and East Asian heritage. The Federation of East European Family History Societies (FEEFHS) website **<feefhs.org/links/Germany/ahnstamm.html>** provides a basic background and history of the card file, and FEEFHS has created traditional A-to-Z indexes of the pedigree files contained within the microfilmed card file. The only way to view the actual pedigree charts, however, is either to visit the Deutsche Zentralstelle für Genealogie (German Genealogical Central Office) in Leipzig or to order individual microfilms from the Family History Library in Utah. Unless you live in Germany, the second option is obviously the way to go. Please note that about 40 percent of the card file focuses on central German families.

GRANDMA's Window

GRANDMA (Genealogical Registry and Database of Mennonite Ancestry)'s Window <www.grandmaonline.org/gw-asp-2/login.asp> is a database of Mennonite ancestry, mostly focusing on lines that originated in former Prussian communities in Poland and former Russian communities in Ukraine. You can search the database after registering and paying a one-time twenty-dollar fee. Click the California Mennonite Historical Society link to register.

Meyers Konversationslexikon (Meyer's Encyclopedia)

This website <www.retrobibliothek.de/retrobib/stoebern.html?werkid=100149> has a digitized copy of *Meyer's Encyclopedia*, which contains all the entries you would expect from an encyclopedia. Most notably, *Meyer's* contains descriptions of individual places and provides some anecdotal information. These descriptions can give you an idea about some of the most prominent aspects of your ancestors' lives (if, of course, you know their village of origin).

Google Books Digitized Gazettes

Google Books <books.google.com> has a large collection of digitized German legal newspapers from the nineteenth century. Try searching *Intelligenzblatt* followed by the name of person you're looking for. These papers generally detailed the transfer of real estate that occurred when someone was emigrating.

JEWISH RECORDS

Until World War II and the Holocaust, many Jews lived in Germany and Eastern Europe. Ethnic Germans often have Jewish ancestors, and these Jewish relatives will show up in civil registers (and even sometimes in Christian church registers when a state church compelled Jews to be recorded there). It's also worth noting that the use of surnames by Jews generally only started when decreed by laws. Here are some websites that provide information about German Jews.

JewishGen's German Jewish Special Interest Group

The JewishGen site <www.jewishgen.org/gersig> has a master list of sorts of websites and databases pertaining to Jews, including those in Germany. In addition to an Internet discussion group for exchange of information about German Jewish genealogy, the site offers many helpful maps, a listing of Jewish newspapers in the German language, and a grid showing when Jews were legally required to take "civil names" (surnames).

Jüdische Friedhöfe in Deutschland
(Jewish Cemeteries in Germany)

This website <www.uni-heidelberg.de/institute/sonst/aj/FRIEDHOF/ALLGEM/index.html>, created by the Zentralarchiv zur Erforschung der Geschichte der Juden in Deutschland (Central Archive for the Research of the History of the Jewish People in Germany) and hosted by the University of Heidelberg website, focuses particularly on the inscriptions of tombstones in Jewish cemeteries across Germany, which can provide very useful information. If you have Jewish ancestors from Germany, this can be a good place to look for names and dates prior to emigration.

International Tracing Service

The International Tracing Service holds many documents concerning victims of the Nazi regime during the Holocaust at an online repository <www.its-arolsen.org/en/homepage/index.html>. The archive contains information about individual prisoners at the extermination and concentration camps, and also has some higher-level documents detailing the operation of one of the most murderous governments the world has ever known. Jewish research in the early- and mid-1900s will likely benefit the most from this research, but the archive also contains information about some of the other populations that were subjugated by the Nazis.

OTHER USEFUL ONLINE RESOURCES

In addition to the many websites this book has investigated for their usefulness in setting a foundation for your research, attachment to one or more of the megasites, or applicability to a common genealogical question, still more unique resources can help German researchers. Whether it's the private certificates that are the hallmark of the Earnest Archives and Library or companies offering DNA testing, your trip through the German online world is not yet complete until you've looked at the rest of these sites.

Archives and Libraries

The Earnest Archives and Library <www.earnestarchivesandlibrary.com/index.php> is "devoted to research of Pennsylvania German genealogy recorded on Fraktur, broadsides, family registers, Bible records, official documents, and ephemera." While it has a relatively narrow focus, the library houses an index of more than thirty thousand Fraktur documents, and if your ancestors lived in the main Pennsylvania German areas, the library may have information about them in its index. The people who run the library have published many books about Fraktur, most of them focusing on one particular family name.

Likewise, the Allen County Public Library Genealogy Center has a guide **<www. genealogycenter.org/pathfinders/guides/German.aspx>** that provides a great way to equip you with a list of the most prominent sources for doing German genealogy research. Ahnenforschung.net **<ahnenforschung.net>** is another good starting point for German family history research. Try searching a family name or place name from the main page, which will take you to a list of relevant forum discussions (mostly in German).

Military Records

Given the historically tumultuous political climate in Europe, war likely played an important part in your ancestors' lives, and records from their service can provide important information for your research. The Johannes Schwalm Historical Association **<www.jsha. org>** is dedicated to the history of the soldiers from Hessen that were hired by the British Crown to help them put down the revolution in the American colonies, a conflict known now as the Revolutionary War. The website lists fully and partially researched soldiers, so give it a browse if you feel that your ancestor may have come to the United States in this way.

For researchers looking for their ancestors in more modern conflicts, the Volksbund Kriegsgräberstätten **<www.volksbund.de/graebersuche.html>** allows you to search for German soldiers who were killed in World War I or World War II. Specifically, this group began as a preserver of German military cemeteries and has been doing so since 1919.

DNA Testing

Many of your genealogical brick walls can be busted by using DNA testing. Family-TreeDNA **<www.familytreedna.com>** is specifically mentioned here because of the Y-DNA tests that it offers. Without getting too scientific, the Y-chromosome is passed from father to son, and, in most cases, is completely unaltered (though over the course of time, mutations occur—otherwise, all men on the planet would have the same Y-chromosome). This is useful for genealogy because it can prove that two men directly descend from the same common ancestor even if records are not available to show it. If you are having trouble getting past an ancestor on your direct male-line ancestry, consider being tested (if you're a man) or having a male member of your immediate family (i.e., father or brother) tested. Your results will be placed in a large database for comparison to other people who have been tested.

Two other types of DNA testing, called autosomal and mitochondrial tests are available through FamilyTreeDNA as well as other vendors such as AncestryDNA **<dna. ancestry.com>** and 23andMe **<www.23andme.com>**. The autosomal test is perhaps the most comprehensive of the three. This tests the reshuffled DNA from both mother and father and, when results are compared to another person's, can estimate the closeness of relationship based on the amount of DNA in common. In contrast, the mitochondrial test ("mtDNA" for short) examines mitochondrial DNA, which is handed down (usually intact) from a mother to her children (male and female) but only passed on further by females; therefore, going back in time, it traces the so-called "umbilical line" of your mother, your mother's mother, your mother's mother's mother, etc. This will help you identify potential maternal ancestors and current relatives, but can't fill in other research gaps.

Miscellany

While these resources may be a bit more "out there," you might find that they solve some of your research questions when other, more reliable sources fail:

- Forschungsstelle für Personalschriften <**www.personalschriften.de/datenbanken. html**>: These databases provide an alternate way to look at death records. The main database is a catalog of German funeral sermons with more than two hundred thousand indexed records. Click GESA, then Registersuche to search for the family name of your ancestors.

- Arbeitskreis Volkszahl-Register <**www.akvz.de/e107_plugins/akvzdb_menu/akvzdb. php**>: Censuses were not very common in Germany, but one place where they occurred regularly is in the areas covered by the modern-day German *Land* of Schleswig-Holstein, near the border with Denmark. The years covered on the website are 1693 to 1864.

- Adoption.com German Adoption Records <**registry.adoption.com/b_adoptee_birth_ country_Germany,1.html**>: If you suspect that one of your ancestors may have been adopted, consult adoption registers to continue to be able to do genealogically meaningful research. This site contains a list of more than one thousand documented adoptions from Germany, as well as who submitted the adoption. These adoptions include some from the period immediately after World War II, useful for adoptees searching for fathers they suspect may have been American soldiers.

KEYS TO SUCCESS

▨ Think outside the box when looking for material to help you with your German ancestry. You might potentially find resources on any website, given how widespread and far-reaching German-speaking immigration has been.

▨ Use resources like period newspapers and military records to fill in gaps in your research.

MAPS

German genealogy can be hard to visualize. With Germany's many border changes over the centuries (and its historic lack of centralization), you might have trouble tracking your ancestors *Heimat* across the years. This section features a number of maps that will help you identify what resources may be available for your ancestors.

The maps included in this appendix (in order) are

- a map of modern Catholic dioceses and archdioceses that you can contact for church records
- maps of modern German *Länder* with both German and English names that you can contact for civil records
- a map of Germany shortly after unification in 1871
- a map showing which Protestant churches are participating in Archion's Kirchenbuchportal project (see chapter 8)

You can find more historical maps online at David Rumsey Map Collection **<www.davidrumsey.com>** and the Library of Congress **<www.loc.gov/maps>**.

CATHOLIC DIOCESES IN MODERN GERMANY

Osnabrück

Münster

Essen

Aachen

Köln*

Limburg

Trier

Mainz

Speyer

Freiburg*

Hamburg*

Hildesheim

Berlin*

Görlitz

Magdelburg

Paderborn*

Fulda

Erfurt

Dresden-Meißen

Würzburg

Regensburg

Bamberg*

Eichstätt

Rottenburg-
Stuttgart

Passau

München-
Freising*

Augsburg

*Indicates an archdiocese

MODERN GERMAN *LÄNDER*, GERMAN NAMES

MODERN GERMAN *LÄNDER*, ENGLISH NAMES

Hamburg

Schleswig-Holstein

Mecklenburg-Vorpommern

Bremen

Lower Saxony

Berlin

Brandenburg

North Rhine-Westphalia

Saxony-Anhalt

Saxony

Thuringia

Hesse

Rheinland-Palatinate

Saarland

Bavaria

Baden-Württemburg

GERMANY AFTER UNIFICATION, 1871

NORDSEE

Provinz
Flensburg
Schleswig
Helgoland
(bis 1890 brit.)
Schleswig
Kiel
Holstein
OLD
Hansestadt
Lübeck
Rostock
Ghzm.
Mecklenburg
Schwerin
SCHWERIN
Bremer-
haven
Hansestadt
Hamburg
Wilhelmshaven
NE
OLDENBURG
Hansestadt
Bremen
Provinz
Hannover
Groningen
Ghzm.
Oldenburg
Aller
Elbe
Bra
Kgr.
Niederlande
Ems
Hannover
Amsterdam
Osnabrück
SL
Magdeburg
Den Haag
Weser
BRAUNSCHWEIG
Schweig
Provinz
DESSAU
Arnheim
Münster
DETMOLD
LD
W
Hzm. Braun
Göttingen
Herzogtum Anhalt
Dortmund
Essen
Provinz
Sachsen
Ruhr
Westfalen
Halle
Leipzig
Düsseldorf
Fsm.
Waldeck
Kassel
Schw.-Sondersh.
Lüttich
Köln
Marburg
GOTHA
SWE
GERA
SA
Rheinprovinz
Bonn
Provinz
Hessen-Nassau
Gießen
SWE
SCG
WEIMAR
SA
CK
Kgr. Belgien
Rhein
Wetzlar
SWE
SR
SWE
Koblenz
GH
MEININGEN
SMG
RJL
Rau
Wiesbaden
Frankfurt
SCG
Mainz
COBURG
Ghzm.
Luxemburg
OLD
DARMSTADT
Main
Trier
Ghzm.
Hessen
Würzbg.
Nürnberg
Luxemburg
Königreich Bayern
Maas
Kgr. Bayern
Regensburg
Verdun
Metz
Baden
KARLSRUHE
Elsaß-Lothringen
Reichsland
Kgr.
STUTTGART
Großherzogtum
Nancy
Mosel
STRASS-
BURG
Württemberg
Isar
Frankreich
Colmar
FHZ
Ulm
Augsburg
Lech
MÜNCHEN
Freiburg
Basel

Memel

Tilsit

Königsberg

Provinz
Ostpreußen

Stolp

Danzig   Elbing

Allenstein

Kolberg

Pommern   **Provinz**
Westpreußen

Graudenz

Stettin

Bromberg   Thorn

Weichsel

Provinz

Warthe   Küstrin   Posen   Warschau

Frankfurt

Posen   **Kaiserreich Russland**

Oder   Glogau

Provinz   Lodz

Liegnitz   Breslau

hsen

Schlesien   Oppeln

Beuthen
Königshütte   Kattowitz

Elbe   Gleiwitz

Prag   Krakau

Moldau   Brünn

Kaiserreich   **Königreich Ungarn**

Linz   WIEN   Preßburg

Österreich

ARCHION KIRCHENBUCHPORTAL PARTICIPANTS

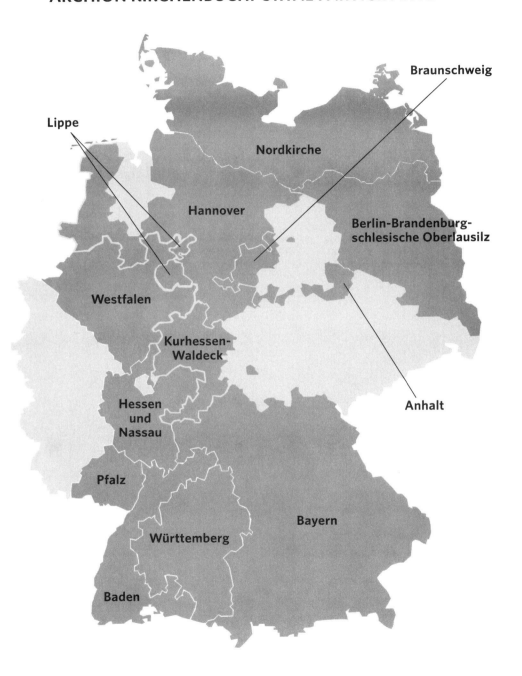

Braunschweig

Lippe

Nordkirche

Hannover

Berlin-Brandenburg-
schlesische Oberlausilz

Westfalen

Kurhessen-
Waldeck

Hessen
und
Nassau

Anhalt

Pfalz

Bayern

Württemberg

Baden

B

WEBSITE INDEX

The Internet can be a wonderful (if not overwhelming) resource for German genealogists, and this guide focuses on the many resources the Internet can offer. This section lists all of the websites discussed throughout the book as well as the chapter in which they appear. And as discussed in chapter 1, you can categorize websites with German genealogical content by what language(s) they're written in. In this appendix, sites are labeled in this way: English (E), German with no translation (G), or German with an English translation or version provided by the website (G/E). Websites can also be categorized based on whether their content is free or requires a subscription; make sure you know what resources a site can offer (and if you can access them anywhere else for free) before you commit money to a website.

The German Genealogy Websites Guide flow chart on the pages that follow will also help you identify the next step in your research. You can download both the site index and the flow chart at <ftu.familytreemagazine.com/trace-your-german-roots-online>.

FLOW CHART: GERMAN GENEALOGY WEBSITES GUIDE

STEP 1 : Framing the Right Question

Identify what stage of research that you're in by formulating a research plan and correctly framing questions (see chapter 1). What's the furthest you've gone in your research?

I'm working my way back to a German-speaking immigrant.

I have the immigrant but not the German hometown (*Heimat*).

I have the immigrant ancestor and the *Heimat*.

STEP 2A: Finding the Immigrant

This stage largely depends on how long ago your ancestors immigrated and what sort of paper trail they left behind. Your research will involve the following:

- naturalizations
- civil vital records
- church registers (baptisms, marriages, and deaths)
- tombstones and obituaries
- US censuses
- family Bibles and registers
- fraternal societies' records
- military records (enlistment, discharge and pension)
- letters from relatives

Once you've found your ancestor, go to step 2B.

STEP 2B: Finding the *Heimat*

Once you've found an immigrant ancestor, you're ready for a crucial step: identifying the exact village. Many of the records groups you've used in tracing previous generations will still be relevant, especially:

- naturalizations
- church registers (baptisms, marriages, and deaths)
- tombstones and obituaries
- family Bibles and registers
- military records (enlistment, discharge and pension)
- letters from relatives

Once you've found both your ancestor and the hometown, go to step 2C.

STEP 2C: Researching the *Heimat* and Beyond

Find records that may mention your immigrant ancestor's family in the old country. Use translation tools (chapter 2) and your knowledge of German phonetics (chapter 3 and the phonetischen Namen Karte chart) to investigate German-language records.

Continue on once you've started to trace your ancestors in Europe.

Go to step 3

Step 3: Building a Profile

To find additional records, you'll being analyzing your immigrant in context of his village. Genealogy.net (chapter 6), organizations (chapter 12), connecting with other researchers through social media (chapter 13), and people and businesses in Germany via *Das Telefonbuch* (chapter 11), can all be helpful.

Your next step will be decided by how thoroughly you've investigated religious records.

I still need to research some religious records.

I'm all out of religious records to search.

Step 4A: Searching religious records

Your immigrant ancestor's religion is important because of the many records that most faith communities have generated. You likely have determined your ancestor's religion in previous steps, and religious affiliation did not change in many families across generations. Most Germans were either:

- Protestant (*Evangelisch*): Search Archion (chapter 8)
- Roman Catholic (*Katholisch;* chapters 10 and 13)
- Jewish (*Jüdisch;* chapter 14)

If church records are not digitized or are with archives, contact the appropriate archive (chapter 11).

Step 4B: Considering political territories

Many German records are more localized than American records due to Germany's history of decentralization. Think in triplicate (*Denken Dreimal*) and use the *Heimat* Tic Tac Toe in chapter 9 to get a snapshot of the three most important times relating to your ancestor's village, including where it was at a particular time in history.

Step 5: Putting German archives to use

Unfortunately, some records are not yet available online. Don't be afraid to reach out to German archives if you're confident they have records you need, especially those relating to geographic areas (chapter 9) and church and civil archives (chapter 12).

LANGUAGE AND TRANSLATION

Site Name	URL	Chapter	Language
About.com: German Language	<www.german.about.com/library/blfunkabc.htm>	3	E
About.com: Old German Script—Kurrent	<www.genealogy.about.com/od/paleography/ig/old_handwriting/Kurrent.htm>	2	E
BabelFish	<www.babelfish.com>	2	E
BEOLINGUS—Your Online Dictionary	<dict.tu-chemnitz.de>	2	E
Deutsche Welle	<www.dw.de/learn-german/s-2469>	2	E
Brigham Young University: The German Script Tutorial	<script.byu.edu/Pages/German/en/welcome.aspx>	2	E
Deutsches Wörterbuch von Jacob Grimm und Wilhelm Grimm	<www.woerterbuchnetz.de/DWB>	2	G
Dict.cc Deutsch-Englisch Wörterbuch	<www.dict.cc>	2	G/E
Duolingo	<www.duolingo.com>	2	E
Family History Library Handwriting Guide: German Gothic	<feefhs.org/guides/German_Gothic.pdf>	2	E
Genealoger: German Genealogy—Language, Handwriting, and Script	<www.genealoger.com/german/ger_german_language.htm>	2	E
Google Translate	<translate.google.com>	2	E
Language Surfer: How to Pass the German A1 Test	<www.languagesurfer.com/2013/08/19/how-to-pass-the-german-a1-test>	2	E
Learn German by Podcast	<www.learngermanbypodcast.com>	2	E
LEO	<www.dict.leo.org>	2	G/E
Linguee English-German Dictionary	<www.linguee.com>	2	E

Site Name	URL	Chapter	Language
Mango Languages	<www.mangolanguages.com>	2	E
MindSnacks	<www.mindsnacks.com>	2	E
My Ancestors and Me: Helps for Translating That Old German Handwriting	<www.nancysfamilyhistoryblog.blogspot.com/2011/06/helps-for-translating-that-old-german.html>	2	E
Omniglot: German	<www.omniglot.com/writing/german.htm>	2	E
National Institute for Genealogical Studies	<www.genealogicalstudies.com>	2	E
Paul Joyce German Course: A Guide to German Pronunciation	<www.joycep.myweb.port.ac.uk/pronounce>	3	E
Slow German Podcast	<www.slowgerman.com/category/absolute-beginner>	2	E
Suetterlin Schrift: German handwriting	<www.suetterlinschrift.de/Englisch/Sutterlin.htm>	2	E
SurvivalPhrases.com: German	<www.survivalphrases.com/german>	2	E

GEOGRAPHY

Site Name	URL	Chapter	Language
Des Atlas des Deutschen Reichs	<uwdc.library.wisc.edu/collections/German/Ravenstein>	3	E
Geogen	<legacy.stoepel.net>	3	G/E
GermanNames	<www.germannames.com>	3	E
Google Maps	<maps.google.com>	3	E
Kartenmeister	<www.kartenmeister.com>	3	E
ViaMichelin	<www.viamichelin.com>	3	E

IMMIGRATION

Site Name	URL	Chapter	Language
Amerikanetz	<www.amerikanetz.de/beitraege/?&no_cache=1&L=0>	9	G
Das Auswander-Archiv Nordfriesland	<www.nordfriiskinstituut.de/indexausw_e.html>	9	G/E
Auswandererliste Rheinenser	<www.rheineahnen.de/listdoc/auswand.htm>	9	G
Auswandererlisten des ehemaligen Herzogtums Braunschweig	<www.thomas-erbe.de/ahnen/buch/001.htm>	9	G
Auswanderung aus dem Rheingau	<www.rheingau-genealogie.de/seite16.htm>	9	G
Auswanderung aus Südwestdeutschland	<www.auswanderer-bw.de>	9	G/E
Auswanderung Neuhauser Bürger	<www.lang-germany.de/Archiv/Auswanderer_/auswanderer_.htm>	9	G
Bremer Passagierlisten	<www.passagierlisten.de>	9	G/E
CUXAUS	<www.hapaghalle-cuxhaven.de/auswandererdatenbank>	9	G/E
Emigration from Lippe to the USA	<www.lippe-auswanderer.de/htm/auswanderer-usa-eng.htm>	9	E
Emigration out of Schleswig-Holstein, 19th century	<www.rootdigger.de/Emi.htm>	9	E
Emslanders to the American Mid-West	<www.emslanders.com>	9	E
Familienbuch Euregio	<www.familienbuch-euregio.eu/guest.html>	9	G
Genealogie und Haus-Chroniken im Gebiet nordwestlich von Münche	<www.genealogie-kiening.de>	9	G
Genealogical Research in Schleswig-Holstein	<www.hans-peter-voss.de/gen/e>	9	E
German Genealogical Research Service Emigrants Database	<www.ggrs.com/emigrants>	9	E
GermanImmigrants1850s.com	<www.germanImmigrants1850s.com>	9	E

Site Name	URL	Chapter	Language
List of Buer Emigrants to the USA	<www.buer-us.de/Book1a.html>	9	E
Mecklenburg Emigrant Database	<www.immigrantgensoc.org/searches/imed/igs-imed.html>	9	E
Militsch-Trachenberg in Niederschlesien	<www.militsch.de>	9	G
Oldenburger Jahrbuch	<www.honkomp.de/damme-auswanderung>	9	G/E
Quellen zur Geschichte von Borgholz und benachbarter Orte	<www.mynetcologne.de/~nc-kornhomi/borgholz2.html>	9	G
Regionale Auswandererdatenbank CLAUS	<routes.de/tinc?key=aDbVINBZ&formname=CLAUS>	9	G
Reinhard Hofer's Bavarian Emigrant Name Index	<home.arcor.de/emigration-research>	9	G/E

MISCELLANEOUS
General Reference

Site Name	URL	Chapter	Language
Adoption.com German Adoption Records	<registry.adoption.com/b_adoptee_birth_country_Germany,1.html>	14	E
Ancestry.com	<www.ancestry.com>	5	E
Cyndi's List	<www.cyndislist.com>	1	E
FamilySearch.org	<www.familysearch.org>	4	E
FamilyTreeDNA	<www.familytreedna.com>	14	E
Geni.com	<www.geni.com>	7	E
GenWiki	<wiki-en.genealogy.net>	6	E
Genealogy.net	<www.compgen.de>	6	G

Site Name	URL	Chapter	Language
German National Tourist Board	<www.germany.travel/en/index.html>	3	E
MyHeritage	<www.myheritage.com>	7	E
One-Step Webpages by Stephen P. Morse	<www.stevemorse.org>	1	E
Rootsweb	<rootsweb.ancestry.com>	5	E
Das Telefonbuch	<www.dastelefonbuch.de>	11	G

Military and Wartime Records

Site Name	URL	Chapter	Language
Die Ahnenstammkartei des Deutschen Volkes	<feefhs.org/links/Germany/ahnstamm.html>	14	E
Fold3	<www.fold3.com>	5	E
International Tracing Service	<www.its-arolsen.org/en/homepage/index.html>	14	E
Volksbund Kriegsgräberstätten	<www.volksbund.de/graebersuche.html>	14	G/E

Death Records and Cemeteries

Site Name	URL	Chapter	Language
Find A Grave	<www.findagrave.com>	1	E
Forschungsstelle für Personalschriften	<www.personalschriften.de/datenbanken.html>	14	G

GENEALOGICAL AND HISTORICAL SOCIETIES

Site Name	URL	Chapter	Language
American Historical Society of Germans from Russia	<www.ahsgr.org/index.htm>	12	E
Board of Certification of Genealogists	<www.bcgcertification.org>	1	E

Site Name	URL	Chapter	Language
German Interest Group—Wisconsin	<www.gig-wi.com>	12	E
The German Society of Pennsylvania	<www.germansociety.org>	12	E
German-Texan Heritage Society	<www.germantexans.org>	12	E
Germanic Genealogy Group	<www.ggsmn.org>	12	E
Germans from Russia Heritage Society	<www.grhs.org/index.html>	12	E
Die Griese Gegend in Mecklenburg	<griesegegend-online.de>	10	G
Herder-Institut	<www.herder-institut.de/en/home.html>	12	G/E
Hessian Regional History Information System	<lagis.online.uni-marburg.de/en>	12	G/E
Homepage der Familie Gschweng aus Greifswald	<www.gschweng.de>	10	G
Institut für pfälzische Geschichte und Volkskunde	<www.pfalzgeschichte.de>	12	G
JewishGen German Jewish Special Interest Group	<www.jewishgen.org/gersig>	14	E
The Johannes Schwalm Historical Association	<www.jsha.org>	14	E
Jüdische Friedhöfe in Deutschland	<www.uni-heidelberg.de/institute/sonst/aj/FRIEDHOF/ALLGEM/index.html>	14	E
Many Roads	<www.many-roads.com/2014/12/14/german-genealogical-societies>	12	E
Die MAUS—Gesellschaft für Familienforschung e. V., Bremen	<www.die-maus-bremen.de/index.php>	12	G
Mid-Atlantic Germanic Society	<www.magsgen.com/index.php>	12	E
Palatines to America	<www.palam.org>	12	E
Pennsylvania German Cultural Heritage Center	<sites.google.com/site/pagermanchc/home>	12	E

Site Name	URL	Chapter	Language
The Pennsylvania German Society	<www.pgs.org/default.asp>	12	E
Rheinland-Pfalz	<www.dilibri.de>	12	G/E
Sacramento German Genealogy Society	<www.sggs.us>	12	E
Society of the Descendants of the Schwenkfeldian Exiles	<www.schwenkfelderexilesociety.org>	12	E
Wittgensteiner Familiendatei	<www.wittgensteiner.net>	10	G/E

ARCHIVES AND CHURCHES

Site Name	URL	Chapter	Language
Allen County Public Library	<www.genealogycenter.org/pathfinders/guides/German.aspx>	14	E
Arbeitsgemeinschaft für mitteldeutsche Familienforschung e.V.	<www.amf-verein.de>	12	G
Archion	<www.archion.de>	8	G/E
Archives Départmentales Du Bas-Rhin	<etat-civil.bas-rhin.fr/adeloch/index.php>	10	n/a (French)
Archives Départmentales Du Haut-Rhin	<www.archives.cg68.fr>	10	n/a (French)
Archivportal	<www.archivportal-d.de>	12	G
Bremische Evangelische Kirche	<www.kirche-bremen.de/index2.php>	12	G
Das Bundesarchiv	<www.bundesarchiv.de/index.html.de>	12	G/E
Deutsche Zentralstelle für Genealogie	<www.archiv.sachsen.de/6319.htm>	12	G
Earnest Archives and Library	<www.earnestarchivesandlibrary.com/index.php>	14	E
Evangelisch-Lutherische Kirche in Oldenburg	<www.kirche-oldenburg.de/?1>	12	G

Site Name	URL	Chapter	Language
Evangelisch-Lutherische Landeskirche in Braunschweig	<www.landeskirche-braunschweig.de/aktuell.html?no_cache=1>	12	G
Evangelischen Kirche in Mitteldeutschland	<archive.ekmd-online.de/portal>	12	G
Evangelisches Zentralarchiv in Berlin	<www.ezab.de>	12	G/E
Katholisch Kirche in Deutschland	<www.katholisch.de/kirche/Deutschland>	12	G
Kirchenbuch Virtuell	<www.kirchenbuch-virtuell.de>	10	G
Lippische Landeskirche	<www.lippische-landeskirche.de/1-4-36>	12	G
Matricula	<www.icar-us.eu/cooperation/online-portals/matricula>	10	G
Moravian Archives—Northern Province	<www.moravianchurcharchives.org>	12	E
Moravian Archives—Southern Province	<www.moravianarchives.org>	12	E
Staatsarchiv Freiburg	<https://www2.landesarchiv-bw.de/ofs21/olf/start.php?bestand=10028>	10	G

SOCIAL MEDIA

Site Name	URL	Chapter	Language
Facebook: Ahnenforschung group	<www.facebook.com/groups/358990344127948>	13	G/E
Facebook: FEEFHS group	<www.facebook.com/groups/278430439787>	13	E
Facebook: Genealogy Translations group	<www.facebook.com/groups/genealogytranslation>	13	E
Facebook: German Genealogy group	<www.facebook.com/groups/GermanGenealogy>	13	E
Pinterest	<www.pinterest.com>	13	E
Twitter	<www.twitter.com>	13	E
YouTube	<www.youtube.com>	13	E

NEWSPAPERS AND PUBLICATIONS

Site Name	URL	Chapter	Language
Allgemeine Auswanderungs-Zeitung	\<zs.thulb.uni-jena.de/receive/jportal_jpjournal_00000025>	14	G/E
Arbeitskreis Volkszahl-Register	\<www.akvz.de/e107_plugins/akvzdb_menu/akvzdb.php>	14	G/E
Bavarica	\<bavarica.digitale-sammlungen.de>	14	G/E
The Berlin Telephone and Address Directories	\<digital.zlb.de/viewer/cms/82>	9	G/E
Chronicling America	\<chroniclingamerica.loc.gov>	14	E
Freiburger Historische Bestände—Digital	\<az.ub.uni-freiburg.de/show/fz.cgi?pKuerzel=FZ>	14	G
Genealogy Bank	\<www.genealogybank.com>	14	E
German History in Documents and Images	\<www.germanhistorydocs.ghi-dc.org>	3	E
German-North American Resources Partnership via WESS	\<www.wessweb.info/index.php/German-Language_Newspaper_Access_in_North_America>	14	E
Google Books	\<books.google.com>	14	E
GRANDMA's Window	\<www.grandmaonline.org/gw-asp-2/login.asp>	14	E
Meyers Konversationslexikon	\<www.retrobibliothek.de/retrobib/stoebern.html?werkid=100149>	14	G
Newspapers.com	\<www.newspapers.com>	5	E
ZEFYS	\<zefys.staatsbibliothek-berlin.de>	14	G

INDEX

Acknowledgments

Many people have played a role in helping me put together this book—too many to name here—but they all have my appreciation. For their significant contributions, my thanks go to: Baerbel Johnson of FamilySearch (and for her breathtaking general knowledge of German genealogy), Fritz Juengling, Terri J. Bridgwater, Reinhard Hofer, Michael J. Hall, Helga Daub, Debra Hoffman, Janell Vasquez (of FamilySearch Indexing), Roger Minert, Kenneth W. Heger, Lisa B. Lee, André Dominguez, Dave McDonald, Michael John Neill, Glen W. Covert, Kory Meyerink, Matthew Deighton (of Ancestry.com), Peter Drinkwater (of Newspapers.com), Diahan Southard (Your DNA Guide), Karen Hägele (of MyHeritage) and Timo Kracke (of Verein für Computergenealogie e.V.)

I'm also extremely appreciative of the attention given this book by publisher Allison Dolan and editor Andrew Koch, as well as the rest of their team at F+W. They have taken my work and made it better every step of the way, from outline to the finished manuscript.

Finally, my special thanks go to Sean Kessler, my associate in James M. Beidler Research and a young genealogist with rapidly growing skills, for his assistance in the production of this volume.

About the Author

James M. Beidler is the author of *The Family Tree German Genealogy Guide* and the award-winning weekly newspaper column "Roots & Branches." He is also a columnist for *German Life* magazine, editor of *Der Kurier*, the quarterly journal of the Mid-Atlantic Germanic Society, and instructor for the online Family Tree University.

James was the president of the International Society of Family History Writers and Editors from 2010 to 2012 and is also the former executive director for the Genealogical Society of Pennsylvania. Beidler frequent contributes to other periodicals, ranging from scholarly journals such as the *Pennsylvania Genealogical Magazine* to popular-interest magazines such as *Family Tree Magazine*. He also wrote the chapter on genealogy for *Pennsylvania: A History of the Commonwealth*, published jointly by the Pennsylvania State Press and the Pennsylvania Historical and Museum Commission. As a lecturer, he was a part of the Pennsylvania Humanities Council's acclaimed Commonwealth Speakers program from 2002 to 2009 and has been a presenter at numerous local, regional, and national conferences. He sits on Pennsylvania's State Historic Records Advisory Board and was a member of the selection committee for the Pennsylvania Digital Newspaper Project. In addition, James is an Enrolled Agent tax preparer and previously was a copy editor for *The Patriot-News* newspaper in Harrisburg, Pennsylvania, for fifteen years.

Beidler was born in Reading, Pennsylvania, and grew up in nearby Berks County, where he currently resides. He graduated Phi Beta Kappa with a BA in political science from Hofstra University in Long Island, New York, in 1982.

Dedication

As with *The Family Tree German Genealogy Guide*, I remember my friend and mentor, the late John T. Humphrey, whose lecture "The 'www' of German Genealogy" was the beginning inspiration for this book.

ISBN: 978-1-4403-4518-0

Other Family Tree Books are available from your local bookstore and online suppliers.
For more genealogy resources, visit **<shopfamilytree.com>**.

20 19 18 17 16   5 4 3 2 1

DISTRIBUTED IN CANADA BY FRASER DIRECT
100 Armstrong Avenue
Georgetown, Ontario, Canada L7G 5S4
Tel: (905) 877-4411

DISTRIBUTED IN THE U.K. AND EUROPE BY
F&W Media International, LTD
Brunel House, Forde Close,
Newton Abbot, TQ12 4PU, UK
Tel: (+44) 1626 323200,
Fax (+44) 1626 323319
E-mail: enquiries@fwmedia.com

DISTRIBUTED IN AUSTRALIA BY CAPRICORN LINK
P.O. Box 704, Windsor, NSW 2756 Australia
Tel: (02) 4577-3555

a content + ecommerce company

PUBLISHER AND COMMUNITY LEADER: Allison Dolan

EDITOR: Andrew Koch

DESIGNER: Julie Barnett

PRODUCTION COORDINATOR: Debbie Thomas

4 FREE
FAMILY TREE TEMPLATES

- decorative family tree posters

- five-generation ancestor chart

- family group sheet

- bonus relationship chart

- type and save, or print and fill out

Download at <ftu.familytreemagazine.com/free-family-tree-templates>

More Great Genealogy Resources

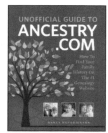

UNOFFICIAL GUIDE TO ANCESTRY.COM

By Nancy Hendrickson

THE FAMILY TREE GERMAN GENEALOGY GUIDE

By James M. Beidler

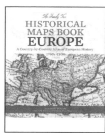

THE FAMILY TREE HISTORICAL MAPS BOOK: EUROPE

By Allison Dolan